Word for Windows® 95
The Visual Learning Guide

Other Prima Visual Learning Guides

Windows 95: The Visual Learning Guide
Excel for Windows 95: The Visual Learning Guide
WinComm PRO: The Visual Learning Guide
PROCOMM PLUS for Windows: The Visual Learning Guide
WordPerfect 6.1 for Windows: The Visual Learning Guide
Word 6 for the Mac: The Visual Learning Guide
Cruising America Online
Quicken for Windows: The Visual Learning Guide
1-2-3 for Windows: The Visual Learning Guide
ACT! 2.0 for Windows: The Visual Learning Guide
Excel for the Mac: The Visual Learning Guide
Windows 3.1: The Visual Learning Guide
Excel 5 for Windows: The Visual Learning Guide
PowerPoint: The Visual Learning Guide
Word for Windows 6: The Visual Learning Guide
WordPerfect 6 for Windows: The Visual Learning Guide
WinFax PRO: The Visual Learning Guide

Upcoming Books!

Sidekick: The Visual Learning Guide
Internet for Windows: America Online 2.5 Edition
Access for Windows 95: The Visual Learning Guide
PowerPoint for Windows 95: The Visual Learning Guide

How to Order:

Individual orders and quantity discounts are available from the publisher, Prima Publishing, P.O. Box 1260BK, Rocklin, CA 95677-1260; (916) 632-4400. For quantity orders, include information on your letterhead concerning the intended use of the books and the number of books you wish to purchase.

Word for Windows® 95
The Visual Learning Guide

David C. Gardner, Ph.D.

Grace Joely Beatty, Ph.D.

PRIMA PUBLISHING

Project Editor: Susan Silva

If you have problems installing or running Word for Windows® 95 (version 7) contact Microsoft at (206) 882-8080. Prima Publishing cannot provide software support.

Prima Publishing and the authors have attempted throughout this book to distinguish proprietary trademarks from descriptive terms by following the capitalization style used by the manufacturer.

ISBN: 55958-737-7
Library of Congress Catalog Card Number: 94-68673
95 96 97 98 AA 10 9 8 7 6 5 4 3 2 1
Printed in the United States of America

Acknowledgments

We are deeply indebted to reviewers around the country who gave generously of their time to test every step in the manuscript. David Coburn, Ray Holder, Jeannie Jones, and David Sauer cannot be thanked enough!

We are especially indebted to Linda Beatty. Her experience, dedication and skills in working with us on many of our Visual Learning Guides have helped us immensely. She was responsible for producing this new version of Word. Linda, we couldn't have done it without you!

We are personally and professionally delighted to work with everyone at Prima Publishing.

J.F. "Cal" Callahan, technical editor; Suzanne Stone, copy editor; Danielle Foster, layout; Emily Glossbrenner, indexer; and Paul Page, cover design, contributed immensely to the final product.

Bill Gladstone and Matt Wagner of Waterside Productions created the idea for this series. Their faith in us has never wavered.

Joseph and Shirley Beatty made this series possible. We can never repay them.

Asher Schapiro has always been there when we needed him.

Paula Gardner Capaldo and David Capaldo have been terrific. Thanks, Joshua and Jessica, for being such wonderful kids! Our project humorist, Mike Bumgardner, always came through when we needed a boost!

We could not have met the deadlines without the technical support of Ray Holder, our electrical genius, Diana M. Balelo, Frank E. Straw, Daniel W. Terhark and Martin J. O'Keefe of Computer Service & Maintenance, our computer wizards!

Contents at a Glance

Customize Your Learning

Prima Visual Learning Guides are not like any other computer books you have ever seen. They are based on our years in the classroom, our corporate consulting, and our research at Boston University on the best ways to teach technical information to non-technical learners. Most important, this series is based on the feedback of a panel of reviewers from across the country who range in computer knowledge from "panicked at the thought" to sophisticated.

Each chapter is illustrated with color screens to guide you through every task. The combination of screens, step-by-step instructions, and pointers makes it impossible for you to get lost or confused as you follow along on your own computer.

LET US KNOW...

We truly hope you'll enjoy using this book and Word for Windows® 95. Let us know how you feel about our book and whether there are any changes or improvements we can make. You can contact us through Prima Publishing at the address on the title page or send us an e-mail letter. Our Internet address is write.bks@aol.com. Thanks for buying the book. Have fun!

David and Joely

WORD FOR WINDOWS 95

Part I: Entering, Editing and Printing Text

Changing Margins and Fonts and Entering Text

The philosophy of the *Visual Learning Guide* series is that people learn best by doing. In this chapter you will:

✔ Open a document
✔ Set margins
✔ Change the font and the font size
✔ Show paragraph formatting marks
✔ Enter text
✔ Learn to read the status bar
✔ Use specialized fonts to insert symbols into the text

OPENING WORD FOR THE FIRST TIME

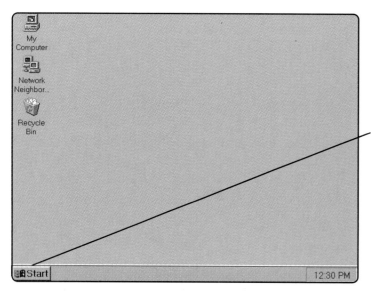

Because Windows provides for tremendous customization, you may have different icons on your screen than you see in this example.

1. **Click** on the **Start button** on the taskbar at the bottom of your screen. A pop-up menu will appear.

2. Drag your **mouse arrow** up to **Programs**. Programs will be highlighted, and a second pop-up menu will appear.

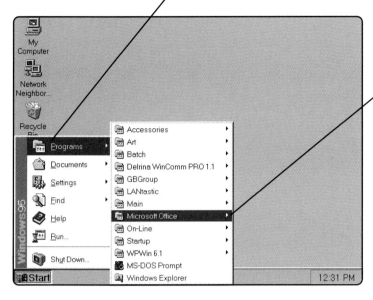

Your pop-up menus may be different than the ones you see in these examples.

3. Drag your **mouse arrow** to the folder that contains Word. In this example, it is **Microsoft Office**. Microsoft Office will be highlighted and a third pop-up menu will appear.

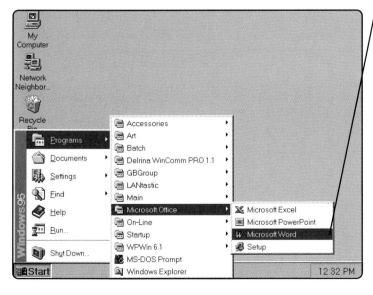

4. Drag your **mouse arrow** to **Microsoft Word**. Microsoft Word will be highlighted.

5. Click the **mouse button.** You will see an hourglass, then the copyright information for Word. Then you will see the opening Word screen.

Notice that the title bar reads Microsoft Word, the name of the person who registered Word 7, and Document1. "Document1" will change when you name the document in Chapter 2, "Naming and Saving a Document."

Notice the following items on your screen:

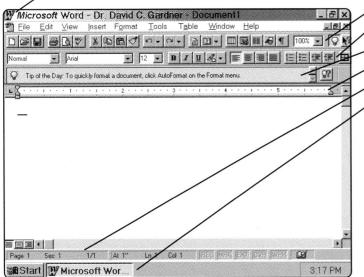

- ◆ Standard Toolbar
- ◆ Formatting Toolbar
- ◆ Tip of the Day Box
- ◆ Ruler
- ◆ Status Bar
- ◆ Taskbar

To give us more room in the Word window, we hid the taskbar for the rest of the examples in this book. If you want to hide your taskbar, follow the directions in Appendix B.

TURNING OFF THE TIP OF THE DAY

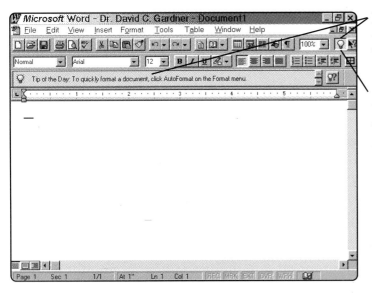

If you *don't* see the Tip of the Day box, click on the TipWizard button now.

1. Click on the **TipWizard button.** The TipWizard button works like a pushbutton. When the Tip of the Day box is on your screen, the button appears pressed in. Click it to close the Tip of the Day box. Click it again to turn it on. Click it once again to turn it off and close the Tip of the Day box.

SETTING MARGINS

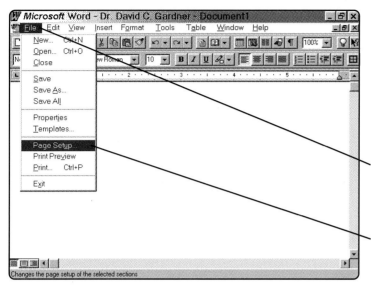

The standard (default) margins in Word are preset at 1 inch for the top and 1.25 inches for the left and right margins. In this example, you will change the top, left, and right margins.

1. **Click** on **File** in the menu bar. The File menu will appear.

2. **Click** on **Page Setup**. The Page Setup dialog box will appear.

You will make the margins smaller than standard to give yourself extra room to create the letterhead in the examples in this chapter. (If you are going to print on stationery that already has a letterhead, the top margin for a short-to-medium-length letter should be about 2.5 inches and the side margins should be 1.25 inches.)

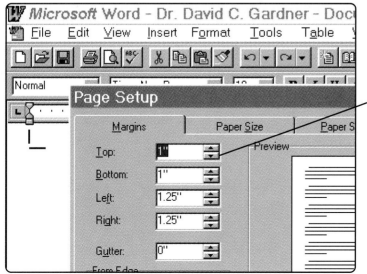

3. **Click twice** on the ▼ next to the Top margin box. The top margin will change from 1 inch to .8 inches.

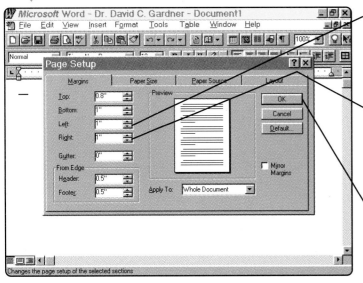

4. Click three times on the ▼ next to the Left margin box until the left margin is 1 inch instead of 1.25 inches.

5. Click three times on the ▼ next to the Right margin box until the right margin is 1 inch instead of 1.25 inches.

6. Click on **OK**. The dialog box will close.

CHANGING THE FONT AND THE FONT SIZE

Word is set to print with the Times New Roman *font*, or type style. In this example you'll learn how to change the font.

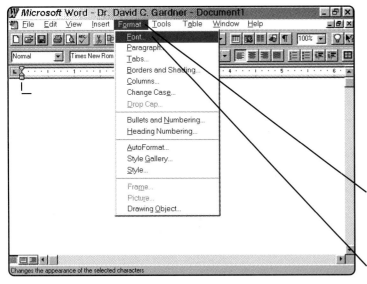

Changing the Current Document Font

The "current document" means the one on your screen. In this example, it's Document1.

1. Click on **Format** in the menu bar. The Format menu will appear.

2. Click on **Font**. The Font dialog box will appear.

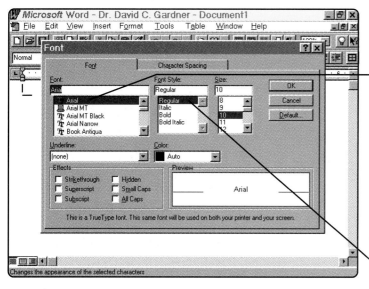

3. **Type** the letter **a** to move to the top of the Font list.

4. **Click** on **Arial** to make your letter look like the examples. If you choose another font, your lines may end differently than you see in the following examples. That's okay. Just be aware that you may see differences.

5. **Click** on **Regular** in the Font Style list if it isn't already highlighted.

Changing the Font Size

Fonts are measured in *points*. Letters are typically written in 10- or 12-point type.

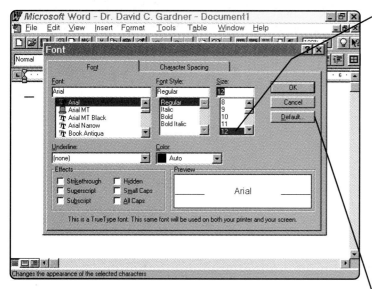

1. **Click** on **12** to make the font larger.

Changing the Font for Future Documents

In the previous section you changed the font for the document on your screen. In this section, you'll make the change apply to all future documents.

1. **Click** on the **Default button** to set Arial with a point size of 12 as the standard settings for all future documents. (These can, of course, be changed or customized any time.)

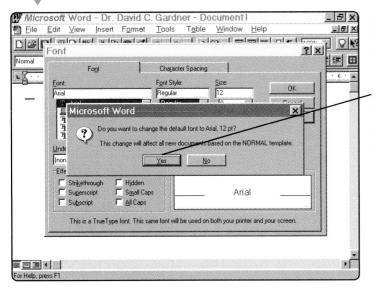

A Microsoft Word message box will appear, asking you to confirm the change.

2. **Click** on **Yes**. The dialog boxes will close, and you will be returned to the Word screen.

Notice the font is Arial and the point size is 12.

You will see a flashing vertical bar (|) at the top of the file. This is called the *insertion point*. It shows where the text will be placed, or inserted, when you begin typing.

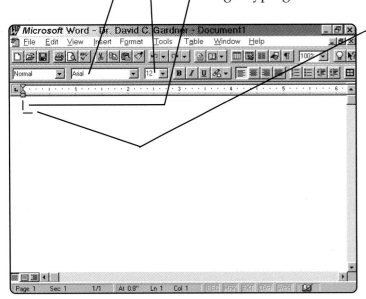

You will also see a horizontal bar (_) below the insertion point. This is called the *end mark*. It will move down the screen as you start each new line of type. It marks the end of the material in the file. Since you haven't entered any text yet, the end mark is at the top of the file.

ENTERING TEXT

Notice that the insertion point is flashing at the beginning of the document. This means you can start typing, and the text will begin at the insertion point.

If you type an incorrect letter, simply press the Backspace key on your keyboard as many times as necessary to erase the incorrect letter(s), then type the letters again.

1. **Type Coburn Costume Company** and **press Enter**.

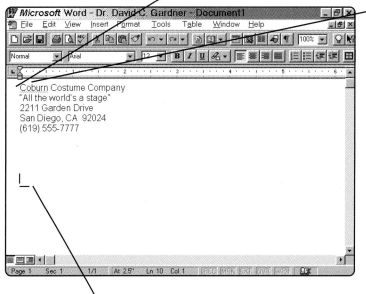

Notice that as soon as you pressed the Spacebar after "Coburn" a wavy red underline appeared. The red line indicates a misspelled or unrecognized word. You'll learn how to correct spelling errors and turn off the underlines in Chapter 3.

Note: If the Tip of the Day box reappears, simply click on the TipWizard button to close it.

2. **Type "All the world's a stage"** and **press Enter**.

3. **Type 2211 Garden Drive** and **press Enter**.

4. **Type San Diego, CA 92024.** (Press the Spacebar twice after CA.) **Press Enter**.

5. **Type (619) 555-7777**.

6. **Press Enter 5 times**. Your screen will look like this example.

Displaying Paragraph, Space, and Tab Symbols

Word can display symbols for paragraphs, spaces, and tabs. It is helpful to see these symbols when you are setting up a document. Even though you can see them on the screen, they will not print.

In this section you will use the Show/Hide ¶ button to display paragraph, space, and tab symbols.

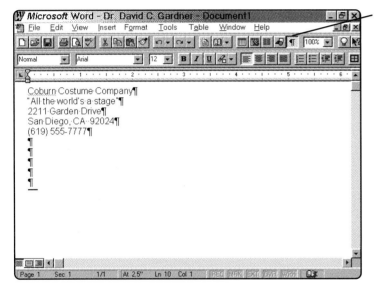

1. Click on the **Show/Hide ¶ (Paragraph) button** on the right side of the toolbar. When you click on the button it appears pressed in. Paragraph symbols (¶) will now appear in the text.

Notice the dots (·) between the words. Each dot represents a space you create by pressing the Spacebar.

Also notice the ¶ at the end of each line and the five ¶ marks at the end of the text. The ¶ appears each time you press the Enter key.

The Show/Hide Paragraph button works like a pushbutton. Click it once to turn it on. Then click it again to turn it off. Click it a third time to turn it on again.

Entering the Date, Address, and Salutation

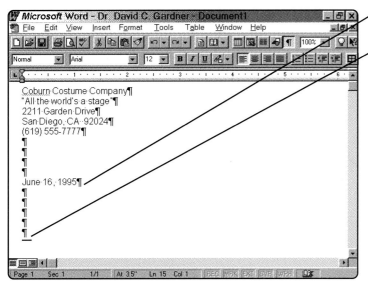

1. **Type** the **date**.

2. **Press Enter 5 times**. Five ¶ symbols will appear.

3. **Type** the following lines. **Press Enter** after each line.

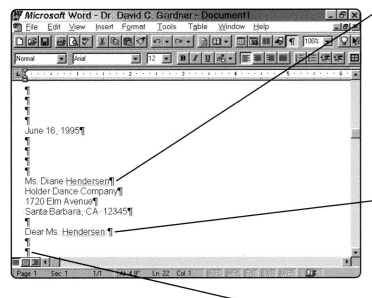

**Ms. Diane Hendersen
Holder Dance Company
1720 Elm Avenue
Santa Barbara, CA 12345**
(**Press** the **Spacebar twice** after CA.)

4. **Press Enter twice** after the last line.

5. **Type Dear Ms. Hendersen:**. (Don't forget the colon.) The screen will automatically move (scroll) up to make room for the additional lines.

6. **Press Enter twice**.

Entering the Body of the Letter

You are now ready to type the body of the letter. Like all word processing programs, you can continue to type without worrying about your right margin. Word will wrap the text around to the next line automatically. Press the Spacebar only once after the period at the end of a sentence. Press Enter only at the end of a paragraph. Press Enter twice to insert double lines after a paragraph.

In word processing programs, a paragraph is considered to be any text that is followed by the Enter command. Therefore, each of the single lines you have already typed is considered an individual paragraph.

1. Type the text below. It contains intentional spelling errors (shown in red). Some errors will be automatically corrected as you type. Other errors will be corrected in Chapter 3. If you make an unintentional typing error, press the backspace key and type the correct letters.

We hope you will be *her* at our Annual Costume Preview on Thursday, July 13, at 2 p.m.

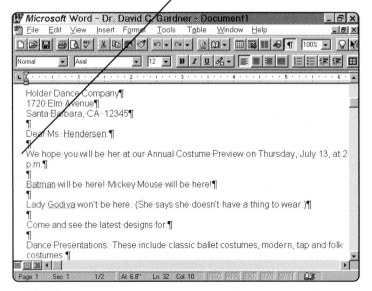

Batman will be here! Mickey Mouse will be here!

Lady Godiva won't be here. (She says she doesn't have a thing to wear.)

Come and see the latest designs for:

Dance Presentations: These include classic ballet costumes, modern, tap and folk costumes.

2. **Continue typing** the following text. Remember, press the Enter key *only* at the end of a paragraph.

Theatrical Presentations: These include costumes for performances such as Cats, Les Miserables, and Phantom of the Opera.

Fantasy Costumes: These include *childrens* and adults' versions of movie characters such as Batman, Catwoman, and Disney characters such as Mickey Mouse.

Historical Figures: These include characters such as Napoleon and Josephine and masks for current political figures.

Pay special attention as you type "*recieve*" in the following paragraph. Word will automatically correct the spelling to "*receive*" as soon as you press the Spacebar. You'll learn about Word's AutoCorrect feature in Chapter 21.

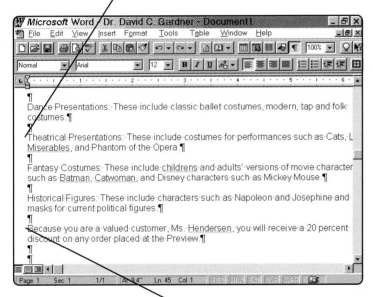

Because you are a valued customer, Ms. Hendersen, you will *recieve* a 20 percent discount on any order placed at the Preview.

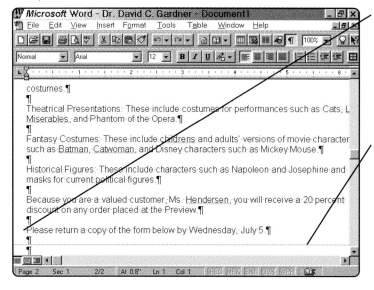

Please return a copy of the form below by Wednesday, July 5.

3. **Press Enter twice** after the last line of type.

Notice the dotted line that appears. This is the *automatic page break*. It indicates the end of the first page. You will change the location of the page break in Chapter 6, "Editing a Document."

The exact location of the automatic page break depends on the margins you set, the size and type of font you use, and your type of printer.

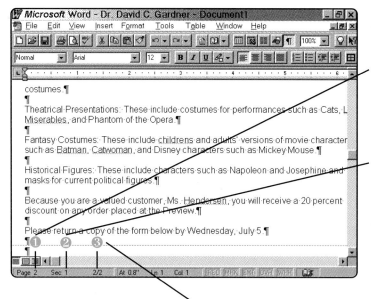

Notice the *status bar* at the bottom of your screen.

❶ **Pg 2** at the far left of the status bar tells you that the insertion point is on page 2 of the document.

❷ **Sec 1** refers to Word's ability to divide a document into sections. Since you haven't divided the document into sections, the entire document will be labeled Sec 1.

❸ **2/2** means that your cursor is on page 2 of a 2 page file (document).

❹ **At 0.8"** means that the cursor is 8/10 inch from the top of the page as it will print.

❺ **Ln 1** means that the cursor is on the first line below the top margin. The exact number of lines on the page depends on the width of the margins and the font size you choose.

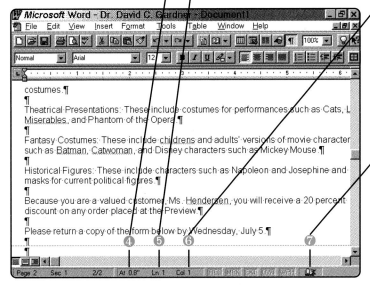

❻ **Col 1** means the cursor is in the first space across the page. The exact number of columns (spaces) that will fit across the page depends on the margins and font size.

❼ This icon is Word's spelling error indicator.

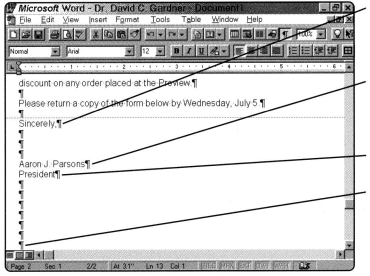

4. **Type Sincerely,**.

5. **Press Enter four times**.

6. **Type Aaron J. Parsons**.

7. **Press Enter**.

8. **Type President**.

9. **Press Enter seven times**. Your screen will look like this example.

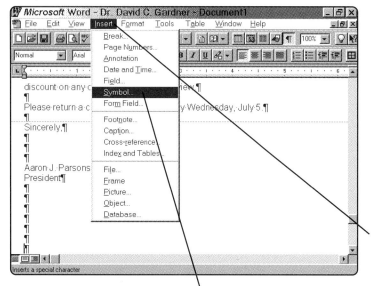

INSERTING A SYMBOL

Windows 95 comes with a number of fonts. One of them, Wingdings, has symbols instead of letters. In this section you will insert a symbol into the text at the position of the cursor.

1. Click on **Insert** in the menu bar. The Insert menu will appear.

2. Click on **Symbol**. The Symbol dialog box will appear.

3. Click on ▼ to the right of the Font box. A list of fonts will appear. The contents of the list depends on the fonts you have installed on your computer. Your list may be different from the one you see in this example.

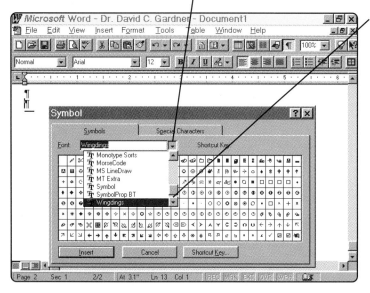

4. Click on ▲ or ▼ to scroll up or down the list until you see Wingdings. (It's possible that Wingdings already shows in the box.)

5. Click on **Wingdings**. The list will disappear, and Wingdings will appear in the Font box. The Wingding symbol set will appear in the dialog box.

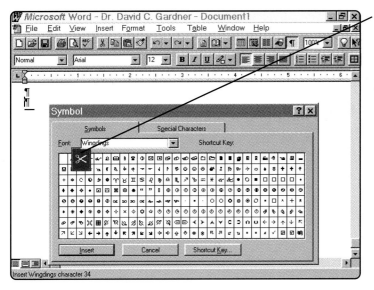

6. Click on the **scissors symbol**, which is in the third position from the left in the first row. The symbol will be enlarged so you can see it better.

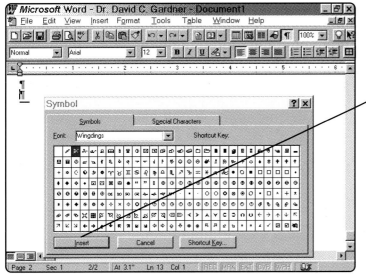

You can repeat step 6 to see other symbols. Make sure to click on the scissors again when you have finished.

7. Click on **Insert**. The scissors will appear in the letter at the insertion point.

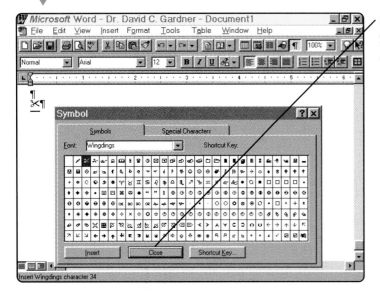

8. Click on **Close**. The Symbol dialog box will close.

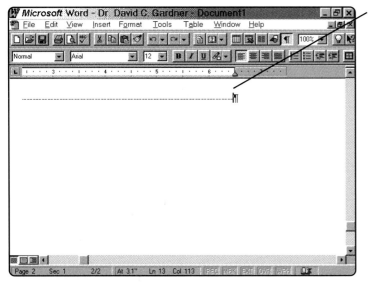

9. Press and hold the **Hyphen key** (-) until the hyphens go all the way across the page. The window will "jump" to the right to show you the right margin. If you go too far, the extra hyphens will wrap around to the next line. Simply press the Backspace key on your keyboard until the insertion point goes back to the previous line.

10. Press Enter twice. The window will return to the left margin view.

11. Type the sentence **I will be attending.** Then **press Enter twice**.

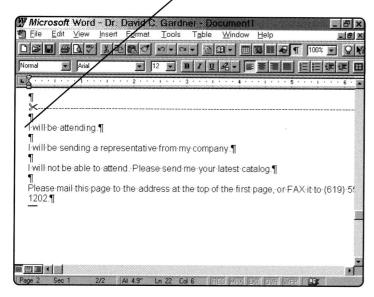

12. Type the sentence **I will be sending a representative from my company.** Then **press Enter twice**.

13. Type the following sentences: **I will not be able to attend. Please send me your latest catalog.** Then **press Enter twice**.

14. Type the sentence **Please mail this page to the address at the top of the first page, or FAX it to (619) 555-1202.**

Congratulations! You just typed your first letter in Word. In Chapter 2, you'll name the letter and save it.

Naming and Saving a Document

Saving a file is as easy as clicking your mouse in Word 7. There's even an Automatic save feature that you can use to save your work at specific intervals. Word is set up to save files to the Winword folder. In this chapter, you will do the following:

✔ Name and save a document
✔ Set the Automatic Save feature to save your document every 10 minutes

NAMING AND SAVING A FILE

In this section you will name the letter you typed in Chapter 1 and save it.

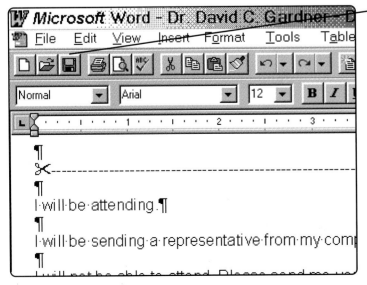

1. **Click** on the **Save button** on the toolbar. Since you haven't named the file yet, the Save As dialog box will appear.

Notice the Winword folder in the Save in text box. This is where your file will be saved.

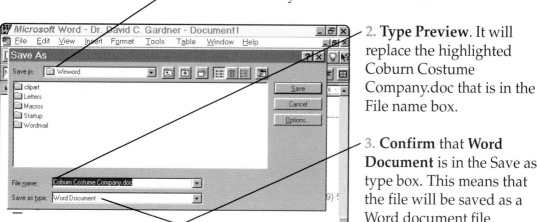

2. Type Preview. It will replace the highlighted Coburn Costume Company.doc that is in the File name box.

3. Confirm that **Word Document** is in the Save as type box. This means that the file will be saved as a Word document file.

SAVING AUTOMATICALLY

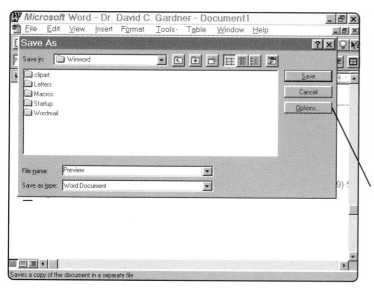

You can set Word to save your work automatically at specific intervals. This does not take the place of a Save command, but it provides a handy backup in case of a power outage or system failure.

1. Click on **Options**.

2. **Click** on the **Save tab** if it's not in the front.

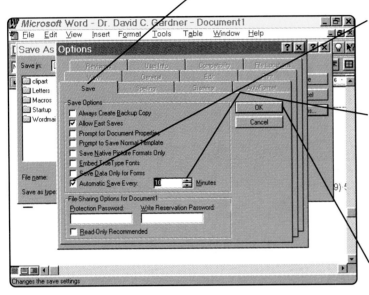

3. **Click** on the **box** next to **Automatic Save Every** to insert a ✔ if one isn't already there.

4. **Click** the ▲ to increase the time between automatic saves. **Click** the ▼ to decrease the time between automatic saves. In this example, the time will be left at 10 minutes.

5. **Click** on **OK**. The Options dialog box will close.

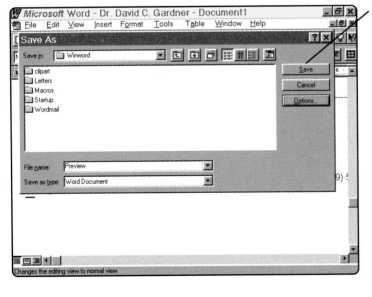

6. **Click** on **Save**. The Save As dialog box will disappear, and the letter will be saved.

Notice that the file name Preview has replaced Document1 in the title bar.

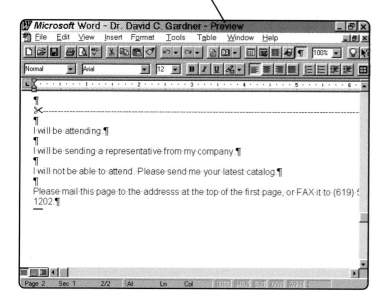

Using the Spelling Checker

Word 7 will mark each misspelled or unrecognized word in your document with a wavy red underline as you type. There are several ways to deal with these errors. In this chapter, you will:

✔ Use the Spelling Checker
✔ Turn off the Automatic Spell Checking

USING THE SPELLING CHECKER

It doesn't matter where your cursor is when you start the Spelling Checker. However, in this example, you'll start at the beginning of the document.

1. **Press and hold Ctrl** as you **press** the **Home key** (Ctrl + Home). This will move the cursor to the beginning of the file.

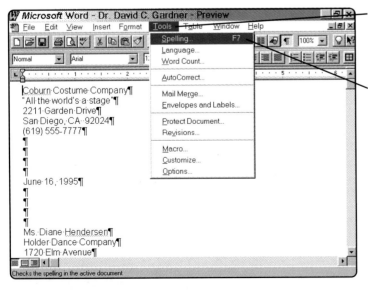

2. **Click** on **Tools** in the menu bar. The Tools menu will appear.

3. **Click** on **Spelling**. The Spelling dialog box will appear.

Notice that Coburn is highlighted in the letter, and the Spelling dialog box is on your screen.

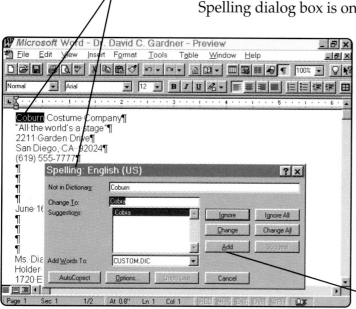

Adding a Word to the Dictionary

Since the company name will be used constantly in your communications, add it to the Custom dictionary. This means that Word will recognize the name in the future and not tag it as a misspelled or unrecognized word.

1. **Click** on **Add**. Word will continue on to the next misspelled word.

Ignoring a Suggested Change

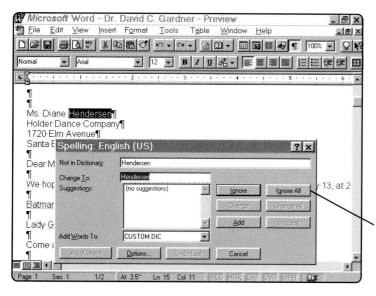

The dictionary is not programmed to recognize most proper names. If the name is one which you will use often, add it to the dictionary as you did above. If you will not use it often, you can choose to ignore Word's identification of it as a misspelled word.

1. **Click** on **Ignore All**. Because Hendersen appears more than once in the letter, this will tell Word to ignore all occurrences of it.

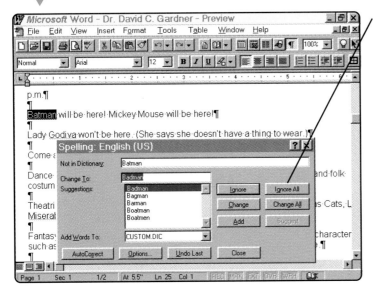

2. Click on **Ignore All** when Word identifies **Batman** as misspelled.

3. Click on **Ignore** when Word identifies the following as misspelled words:
- ❖ **Godiva**
- ❖ **Les**
- ❖ **Miserables**

Correcting a Spelling Error

When Spelling Check identifies a misspelled word, it suggests a list of possible changes.

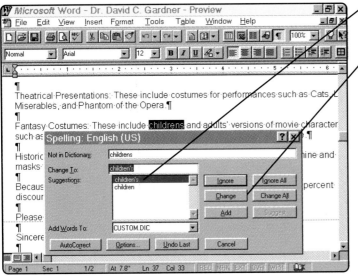

1. Click on **children's** to highlight it, if necessary.

2. Click on **Change**. Word will correct the error and move to the next error.

3. Click on **Ignore** when Word identifies Catwoman as a misspelled word.

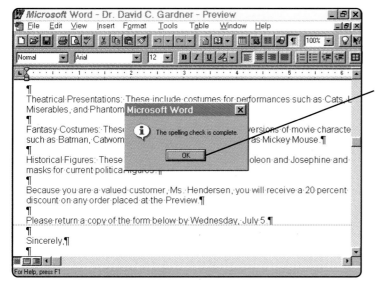

When the spelling check is complete, a dialog box will appear.

4. Click on **OK**. The dialog box will close.

TURNING OFF THE AUTOMATIC SPELL CHECKING

If you find the red underlines annoying, you can turn off the automatic spell checking. It will remain off for all future documents until you turn it on again.

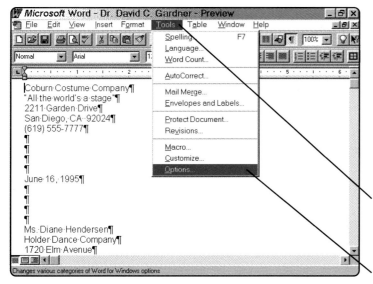

1. Click anywhere on the document to remove the highlighting.

2. Press and hold Ctrl as you **press** the **Home key** (Ctrl + Home) to move the cursor to the beginning of the file.

3. Click on **Tools** in the menu bar. The Tools menu will appear.

4. Click on **Options**. The Options dialog box will appear.

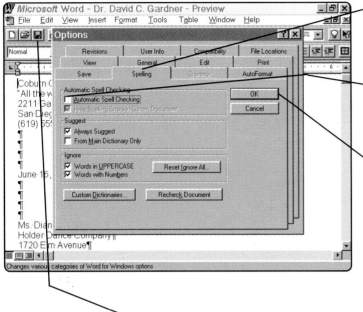

5. **Click** on the **Spelling tab** to bring it to the front, if necessary.

6. **Click** on **Automatic Spell Checking** to *remove* the ✔ from the box.

7. **Click** on **OK**. The dialog box will close, and the Automatic Spell Checking will be turned off.

To replace the Automatic Spell Checking, repeat steps 3 through 7 and put the check back in the box.

8. **Click** on the **Save button** on the toolbar to save your work.

Holder·Dance·Company¶
1720·Elm·Avenue¶
Santa·Barbara,·CA··12345¶
¶
Dear·Ms.·Hendersen:¶
¶
We·hope·you·will·be·her·at·our·Annual·Costum
p.m.¶
¶
Batman·will·be·here!·Mickey·Mouse·will·be·her
¶
Lady·Godiva·won't·be·here.·(She·says·she·doe
¶
Come·and·see·the·latest·designs·for:¶
¶

Notice that Word did not identify "her" in the first sentence as a misspelled word. This is because "her" is a word. It is incorrectly spelled only in the context of this sentence. Computers are not ready to take over the world just yet.

In Chapter 6, "Editing a Document," you will correct this error and make other changes in the letter.

Previewing and Printing a Document

There are several ways to print a document in Word 7. You can print the whole document, the current page, or selected pages. But before you actually print a file, you can take advantage of the Print Preview feature to see how the document will look on the printed page. In this chapter, you will do the following:

✔ Preview a document before printing it
✔ Print a document

VIEWING A DOCUMENT BEFORE PRINTING

In this section you will use the Print Preview button on the toolbar to view a document before printing. If you don't have the Preview file open, open it now.

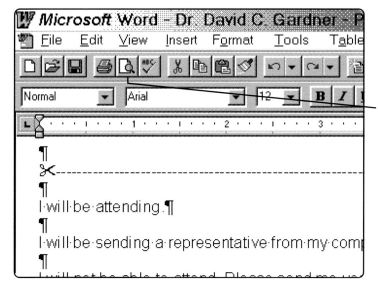

1. **Press and hold** the **Ctrl key** and then **press** the **End key** (Ctrl + End) to go to the end of the file on page 2.

2. **Click** on the **Print Preview button**. The Print Preview screen will appear showing you the page on which your cursor is located.

Magnifying the View in Print Preview

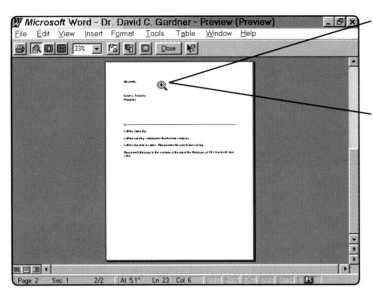

Notice that your mouse pointer is in the shape of a magnifying glass with a little + sign in it.

1. **Click anywhere** on the page. A magnified view of page 2 will appear on your screen.

Notice that instead of the + inside the magnifying glass there is now a - sign.

2. **Click once** to zoom out to a Full Page view again.

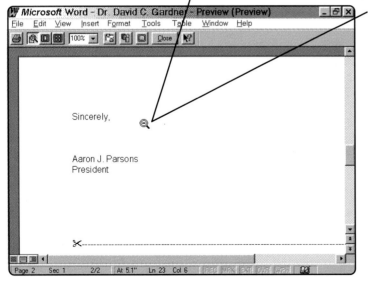

Viewing Multiple Pages in Print Preview

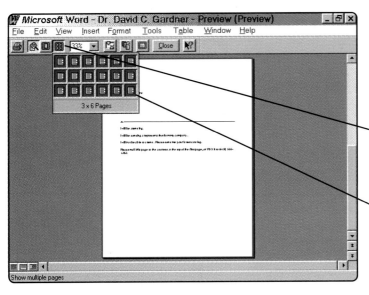

So far you have seen only one page in Print Preview. With the Multiple Page button you can see up to eighteen pages at one time.

1. **Click** on the **Multiple Page button**. A menu will appear.

2. **Press and hold** on any page, then **drag** the **mouse arrow** down and to the right. The menu will expand as you drag to include up to eighteen pages.

3. **Release** the **mouse button** when the number of pages you want to view is highlighted. The pages will shrink to accommodate the number of pages you've chosen.

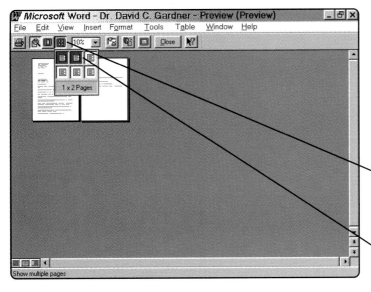

Displaying Two Pages

Our document is only two pages long, so in this example, we'll display the entire document.

1. **Click** on the **Multiple Page button**. A menu will appear.

2. **Click** on the **second page**. This will display two pages of the document.

Changing Pages in Preview

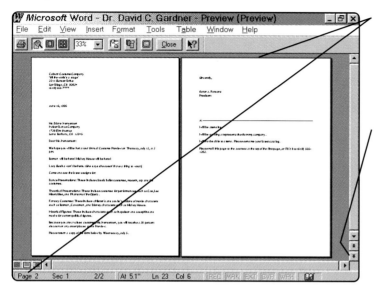

Notice the border around page 2. Notice also that Page 2 shows in the status bar. This is the page where your cursor is located.

If you had more than two pages in your document you would click on the ▼ at the bottom of the scroll bar. This would display pages 3 and 4.

PRINTING WITH THE PRINT BUTTON

In this section you'll use the Print button to print the entire file with a click of your mouse.

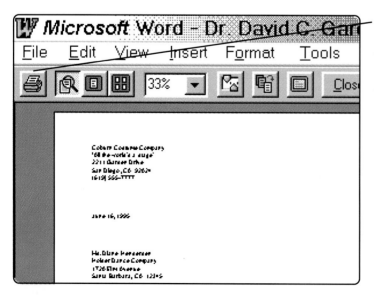

1. **Click** on the **Print button**. A series of dashes will flash by on your status bar to indicate that your file is being sent to your printer.

That's it! That's all there is to printing your entire document!

Closing Print Preview

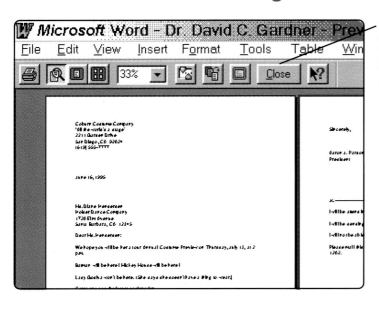

1. **Click** on **Close** to close Print Preview. You will return to the Normal View screen.

PRINTING FROM THE MENU BAR

In this section you will use the Print command on the File pull-down menu.

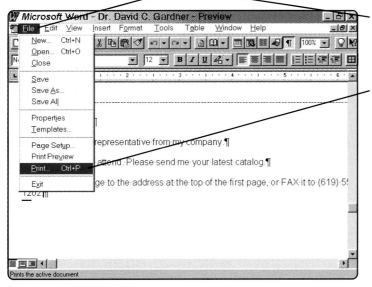

1. **Click** on **File** in the menu bar. The File menu will appear.

2. **Click** on **Print**. The Print dialog box will appear.

Printing Selected Pages

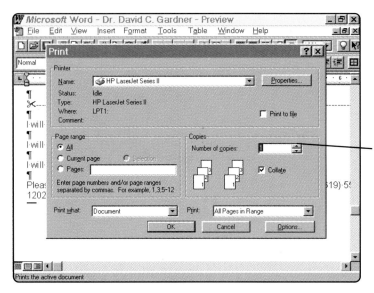

In this section you will not actually make any of the following changes in the Print dialog box, but you should be aware of the options available to you.

Notice that you can change the number of copies you want to print by clicking on the up arrow in the Number of copies box.

Notice that you can print only the page where the cursor is located by clicking on Current page.

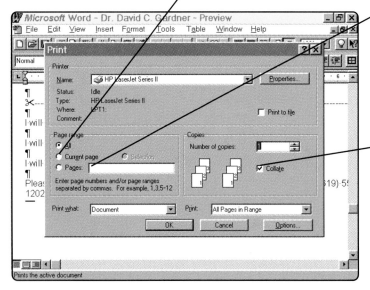

Notice that you can print specific pages by typing page numbers separated by commas. You can also type a range of pages. For example 1-4,7,9,17-20.

Notice that there is a ✔ in the box beside Collate copies. This means that multiple copies will be automatically collated (put in order) as they print.

If you do make any of the above changes, click on OK to print.

Printing the Entire Document

In this section you'll print all of the pages in the document.

1. **Click** on **All** to insert a dot in the circle if one isn't already there.

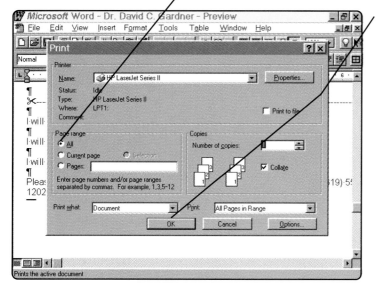

2. **Click** on **OK**. The Print dialog box will close, and your document will be sent to your printer.

Closing a File and Opening a Saved File

Because Word 7 for Windows 95 is a Windows-based program, it uses standard Windows commands to open and close files. As in all Windows programs, there are several ways to open and close files. In this chapter, you will do the following:

✔ Close a file
✔ Close Word
✔ Learn two ways to open a saved file

SAVING AND CLOSING A FILE

In this section you will close the Preview file you created in Chapter 1. Even though you saved the file in Chapter 2, these procedures will start with saving the file. Saving often is a good habit to develop.

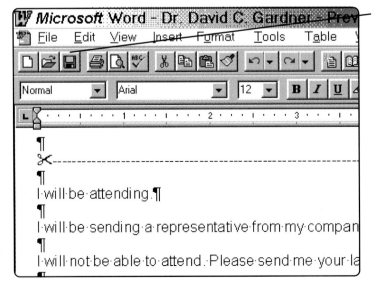

1. **Click** on the **Save button** on the toolbar.

The hourglass will appear briefly along with a series of dashes in your status bar to indicate the percent of the file saved. You won't see any other differences in your screen, but the file and any changes are now saved. Since you already saved the file, you will not see the Save As dialog box.

Closing a File

1. **Click** on **File** in the menu bar. The File menu will appear.

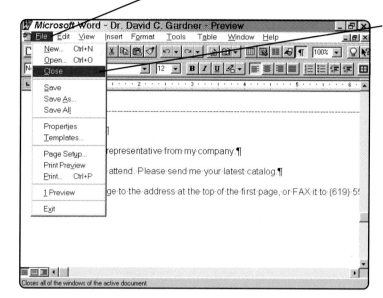

2. **Click** on **Close**. The file will close, and you will see a blank Word screen.

CLOSING WORD FOR WINDOWS

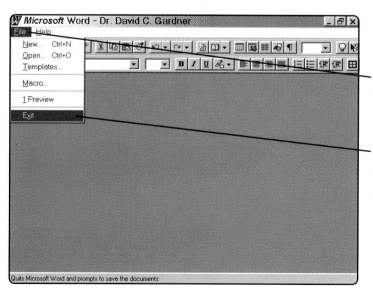

In this section you will close the Word program.

1. **Click** on **File** in the menu bar. The File menu will appear.

2. **Click** on **Exit**. Word will close, and you will be back at the desktop.

BOOTING UP WORD

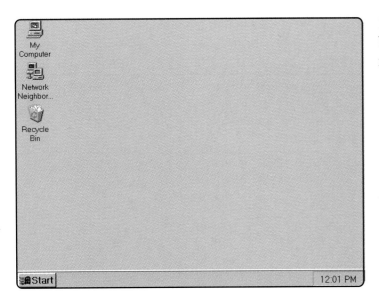

1. **Repeat steps 1-5** at the **beginning of Chapter 1** to reopen Word.

The Tip of the Day box will appear on your screen unless you have turned this feature off as shown in Chapter 1.

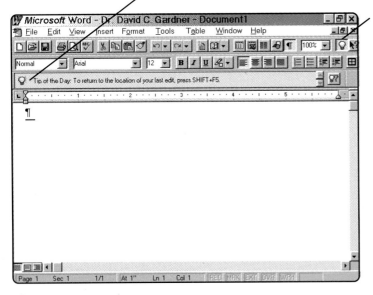

2. **Click** on the **TipWizard button** to close the Tip of the Day box, if necessary.

OPENING A SAVED FILE

There are several ways to open a saved file. In Method #1, you will use the File menu.

Method #1

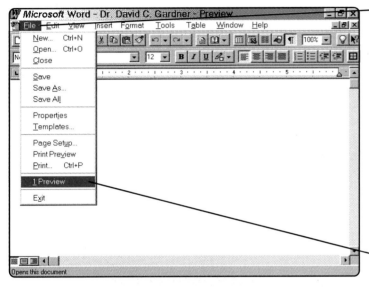

1. **Click** on **File** in the menu bar. The File menu will appear.

The File menu lists the four most recent files you have opened. If you have a new Word 7, there will be only one file listed. If others have used Word before you, you may see up to four files listed.

2. **Click** on **Preview** in the file list. The file will appear on your screen.

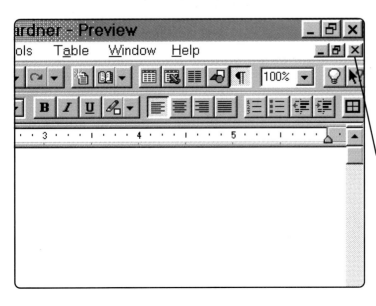

Method #2

Method #2 uses the Open button in the toolbar. In order to try this method, you will close Preview.

1. **Click** on the **Close Document button** to the right of the toolbar. Be careful not to click on the larger Close Word button above it. Preview will close, and you will see an empty Word screen.

2. **Click** on the **Open button** in the toolbar. The Open dialog box will appear.

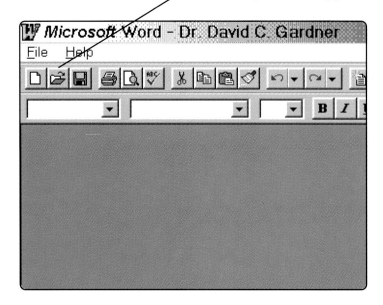

Notice that the Winword folder is in the Look in text box.

3. **Click twice** on **Preview** in the File list. (You can also click once on Preview to highlight it, then click on Open.) The file will appear on your screen.

In the next chapter you will learn how to edit the Preview file.

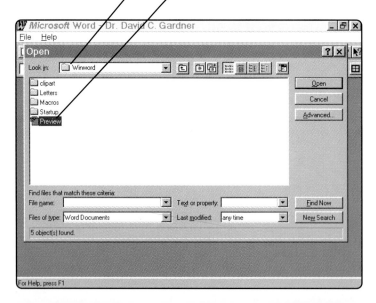

Editing a Document

If this is the first time you have used a Windows-based word processing program, you will be delighted at how easily you can edit a document. Word 7 for Windows 95 has even improved on standard Windows editing commands by adding special features such as drag-and-drop moving and Edit Undo. In this chapter, you will do the following:

✔ Add and delete letters and words and combine paragraphs
✔ Use the Edit Undo feature
✔ Use the Replace All command to correct an error that occurs in several places
✔ Move and copy text
✔ Insert and change the position of the page break

ADDING LETTERS AND WORDS

In this section, you'll make a number of corrections to the letter. The first will be to change "her" to "here."

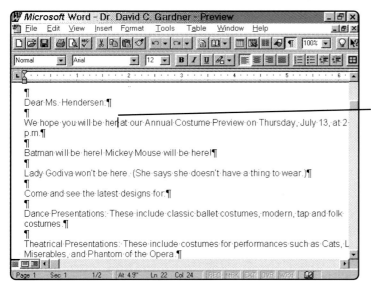

1. **Click** on the ▼ on the scroll bar to bring the first line in the body of the letter into view.

2. **Place** the **mouse pointer** at the **end** of "**her.**" Notice that the mouse pointer is in the shape of an I-beam when it is in the letter. **Click** to set it in place.

3. **Type** the letter **e**. The word will become "here."

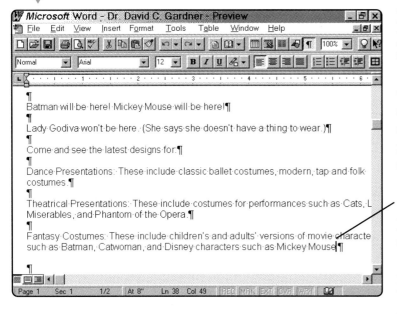

In the next three steps, you'll add words to the end of a sentence.

4. Click on the ▼ on the scroll bar until you can see the two lines beginning with "Fantasy Costumes."

5. Place the **mouse pointer** at the **end** of the sentence **between** "**Mouse**" and **the period. Click** the **mouse button** to set the insertion point in place.

6. Press the **Spacebar** then **type** the words **and Donald Duck**. Notice that the period moves as you add words.

DELETING AND REPLACING WORDS AND COMBINING PARAGRAPHS

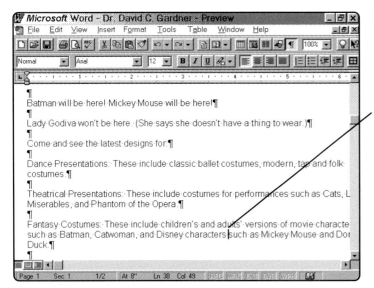

In this section, you will delete unnecessary words.

Deleting Words

1. Place the I-beam to the **left** of "**such as**."

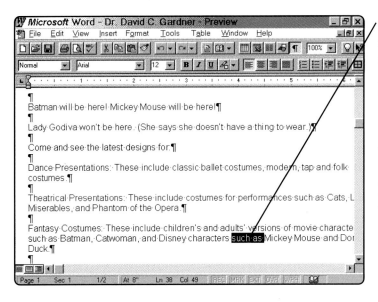

2. Press and hold the **mouse button** and **drag** the **mouse pointer over** "such as" and the **space after as**. They will be highlighted.

3. Release the **mouse button**, then **press** the **Backspace key** on your keyboard. The highlighted words will disappear.

Undoing an Edit

What if you decide you don't want to delete those words? Word has an Undo feature that makes it easy for you to change your mind as long as you haven't done anything else after deleting the words.

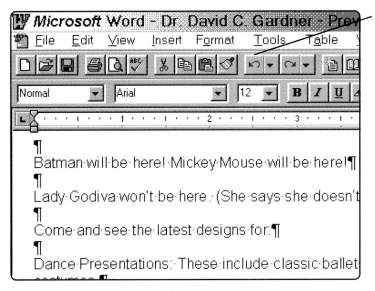

1. Click on the **Undo button** in the toolbar. The deleted words will be restored to the text.

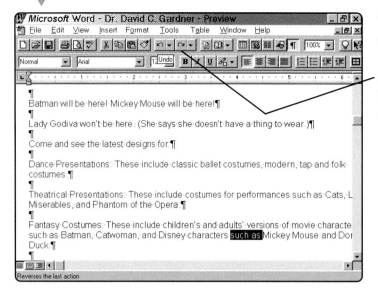

To undo the undo is just as easy.

2. Click on the **Redo button** in the toolbar. "such as" will be deleted again.

Combining Paragraphs

In this section, you will put the Lady Godiva sentences into the preceding paragraph with Batman and Mickey Mouse.

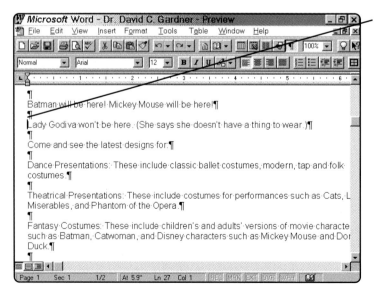

1. Place the **mouse pointer** at the **beginning** of the "**Lady Godiva**" sentence. Make sure that it is in the shape of an I-beam. If the pointer turns into an arrow, move the cursor closer to the words. **Click** to set the cursor in place.

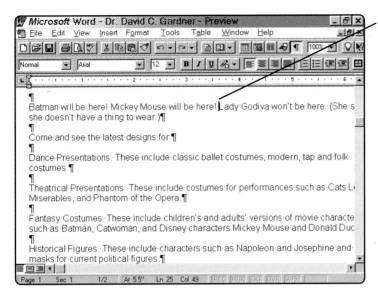

2. **Press** the **Backspace key twice** then **press** the **Spacebar**. This will bring the entire Lady Godiva paragraph up to the end of the Mickey Mouse sentence and put a space between the sentences.

INSERTING A SOFT RETURN

In the example you see here, it would look better if "Les" was on the same line with "Miserables." If you press the Enter key, however, you will insert a paragraph mark (called a *hard return*) and make the second line a separate paragraph. You can, however, move "Les" to the next line with what is called a *soft return*. Unlike hard returns, soft returns are not recognized as paragraph endings in Word.

1. **Place** the **mouse pointer** to the **left** of "**Les**," after the dot. **Click** to set it in place.

2. **Press** the **Backspace key** to delete the space before "Les."

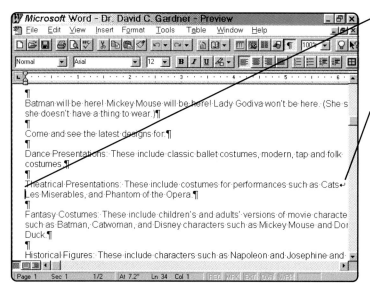

3. **Press and hold** the **Shift key** as you **press Enter** (Shift + Enter). "Les" will move to the next line.

Notice the symbol indicating a soft return at the end of the line.

4. **Press and hold** the **Ctrl key** as you **press End** (Ctrl + End). This will take you to the end of the file.

INSERTING A HARD RETURN

In this example, you will use a hard return to change the spacing in the very last line of the letter.

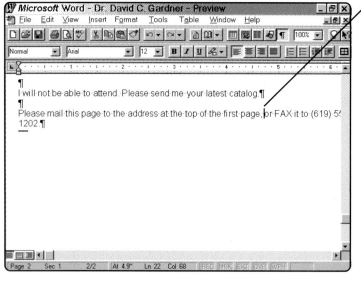

1. **Click** to the **left** of **"or"** in the last line of the letter.

2. **Press** the **Backspace key** to delete the space before "or."

3. **Press Enter**. This will move the cursor and the following text to the next line. These will now be two separate paragraphs.

USING THE REPLACE COMMAND

In this example you will replace "sen" at the end of "Hendersen" with "son." You can replace each "sen" individually or you can use the Replace command to find and replace each occurrence automatically. You will start at the top of the file since the Replace command begins at the cursor and goes to the end of the file.

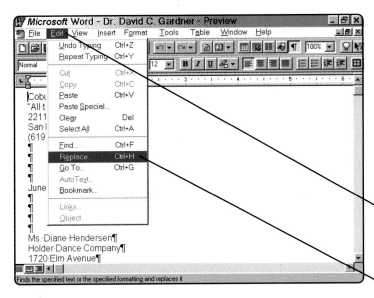

1. **Press and hold** the **Ctrl key** and **press** the **Home key** (Ctrl + Home) to go to the beginning of your file.

2. **Click** on **Edit** in the menu bar. The Edit menu will appear.

3. **Click** on **Replace**. The Replace dialog box will appear. The cursor will be flashing in the Find What box.

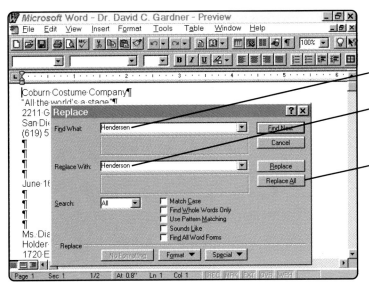

4. **Type Hendersen**.

5. **Click** in the **Replace With box** and **type Henderson**.

6. **Click** on **Replace All**. A series of dashes will appear in your status bar as Word makes all the changes. (See the *User's Guide* for more details about the Replace command.)

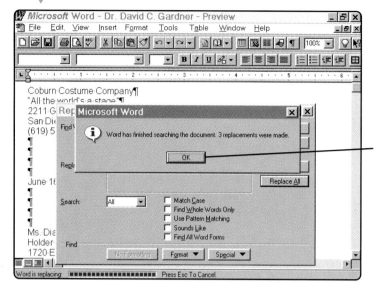

When Word is finished replacing the text, a Microsoft Word message box will appear telling you how many replacements were made.

7. **Click** on **OK** to close the message box. You will see the Replace dialog box.

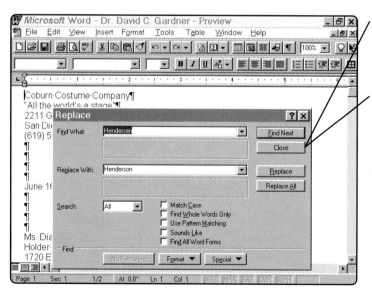

Notice that the Cancel button in the Replace dialog box has changed to Close.

8. **Click** on **Close**. The dialog box will disappear, and the letter will be on your screen with all corrections made. Pretty neat, don't you think?

DRAG-AND-DROP MOVING

In this section you will move the first sentence to a different spot in the letter.

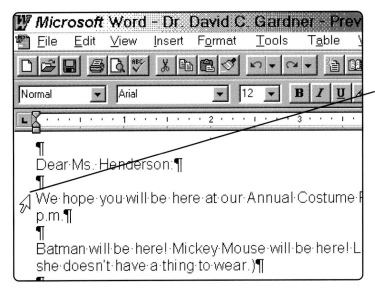

1. **Click** on ▼ to scroll down so you can see the first three or four paragraphs.

2. **Place** the **mouse pointer** in the left margin **beside** the **first paragraph.**

3. **Click twice**. The entire sentence will be high-lighted. (If you click once only the single line beside the arrow will be highlighted.)

4. **Place** the **mouse pointer on top** of "**We**."

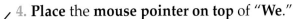

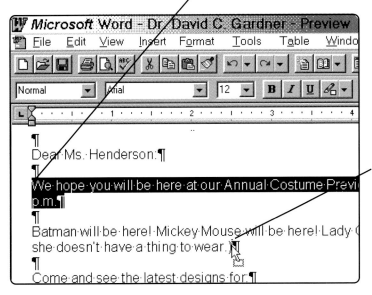

5. **Press and hold** the **mouse button** and **drag** the pointer down to the **end** of the **next paragraph**. You will see a dotted insertion point and a small square being dragged by the arrow.

6. **Place** the **dotted insertion point** to the **left** of the **paragraph symbol,** and **release** the **mouse button**. The paragraph will be moved to that spot.

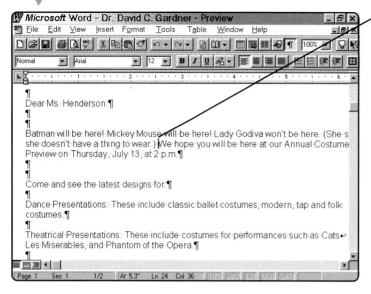

7. **Click** to the **left** of "**We hope**." The highlighting will disappear, and you will see the flashing insertion point.

8. **Press Enter twice** to insert a double space between the end of the "Batman" paragraph and the "We hope" paragraph.

Notice that there is now an extra paragraph mark (and a blank line) at the beginning of the letter.

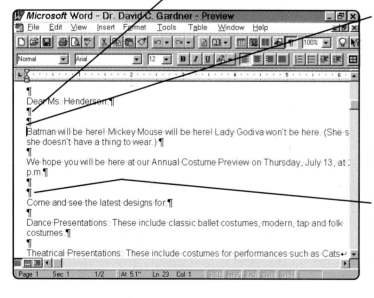

9. **Place** the **mouse pointer** at the **beginning** of the "**Batman**" sentence. **Click** to set it in place.

10. **Press** the **Backspace key once**. The sentence is moved up one line, and the blank line is removed.

11. **Repeat steps 9 and 10** to remove the blank line above the "Come and see" sentence.

INSERTING A PAGE BREAK

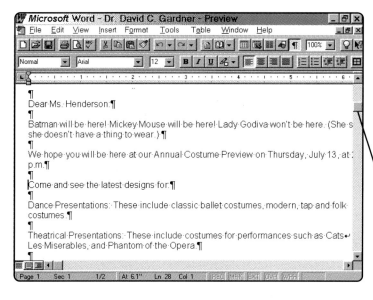

Word does not necessarily insert an automatic page break in a place that makes sense within the context of the document. Fortunately, it's easy to change the position of the page break.

1. **Press and hold** on the **scroll button** and **drag** it halfway down the scroll bar. This will bring you halfway through the document, and you will be able to see the automatic page break.

2. **Click** to the **left** of the "**Please return**" sentence.

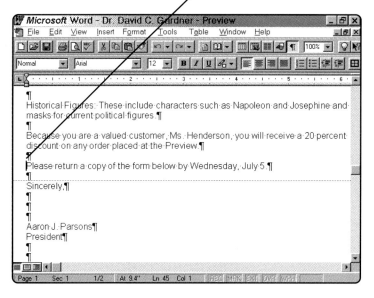

3. **Press and hold** the **Ctrl key** as you **press Enter**. A page break will be inserted into the letter at the insertion point.

When you insert a page break into the text, the automatic page break disappears.

Changing the Position of a Page Break

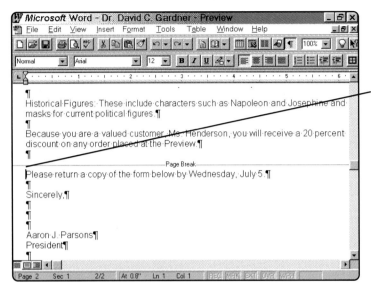

In this example you will delete the page break you just inserted.

1. Click to the **left** of the **first sentence after** the **page break**. If you have been following along, your cursor is already there.

2. Press the **Backspace key**. The page break will be deleted, and the automatic page break will appear again.

3. Click on the **Undo button** to reinsert the permanent page break.

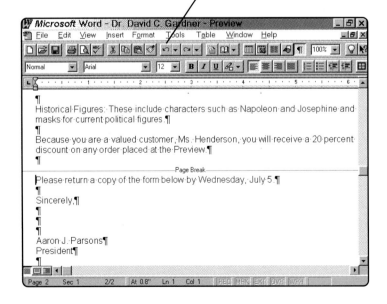

COPYING AND PASTING TEXT

In this section you will learn two ways to copy text from one section of a document to another.

Copying and Pasting Text with the Edit Menu

In this example you will copy text from page 1 of the letter onto page 2.

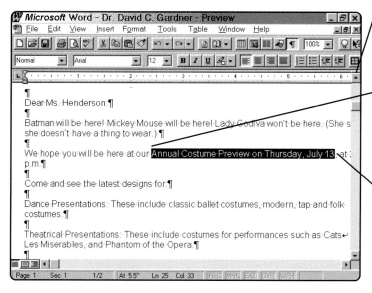

1. **Click** on ▲ to scroll up so you can see the salutation on page 1.

2. **Place** the **mouse pointer** to the **left** of "**Annual Costume Preview.**" **Click** to set the cursor in place.

3. **Press and hold** the **mouse button** and **drag** the cursor **over** "**Annual Costume Preview on Thursday, July 13.**" The words will be highlighted.

4. **Release** the **mouse button**.

5. **Click** your **right mouse button**. A quick menu will appear.

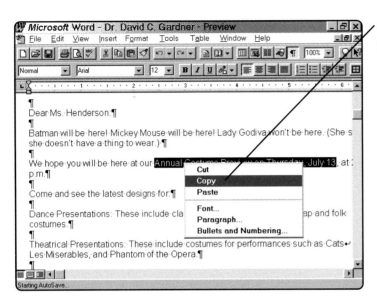

6. **Click** on **Copy**. You will not see any change in your screen, but the highlighted text is now copied to the Clipboard. It will stay there until it is replaced by text from another Copy command.

7. **Press and hold** the **Ctrl key**, then **press** the **End key** (Ctrl + End).

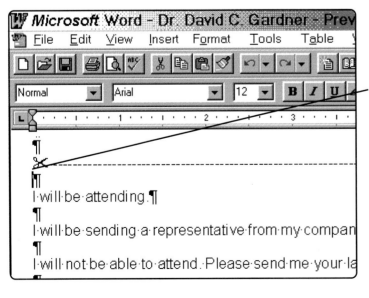

8. **Click** on the ▲ on the scrollbar until you can see the scissors.

9. **Place** the **mouse pointer** to the **left** of the **paragraph symbol** just below the scissors. **Click** to set the cursor in place.

10. **Click** your **right mouse button**. A quick menu will appear.

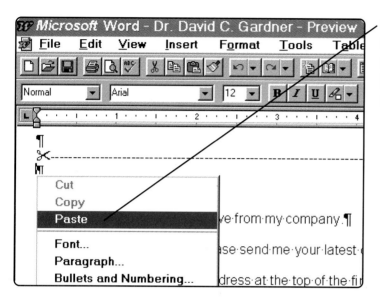

11. **Click** on **Paste**. The text that you copied to the Clipboard will be copied into the document starting at the insertion point.

12. **Click** to the **left** of "**on**" to set the cursor in place.

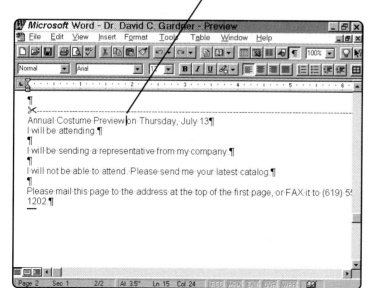

13. **Press Enter** to move "on Thursday, July 13" to the next line.

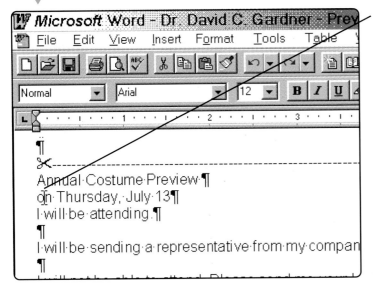

14. **Place** the **mouse pointer on top** of the word **"on."** The pointer will turn into an I-beam.

15. **Click twice.** This will highlight the entire word and the space after it. (This is a handy way to highlight a single word.)

16. **Press** the **Delete key.** The highlighted text will be deleted.

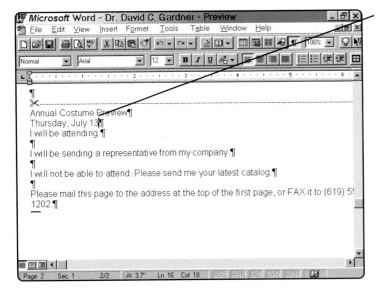

17. **Place** the **mouse pointer** to the **left** of the **paragraph symbol** at the **end** of **"July 13."** **Click** to set in place.

18. **Press Enter twice** to insert two blank lines after the date.

Using the Copy Button

In this three-part example, you'll use the Copy and Paste buttons to copy Ms. Henderson's name and address on the first page and place it on the return form on the second page. First, you'll copy the text.

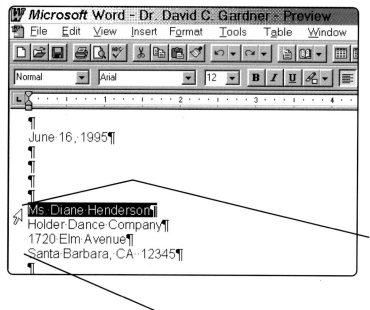

1. **Press and hold** the **Ctrl key**, then **press** the **Home key** (Ctrl + Home) to go to the top of the file. Then scroll down until you can see Ms. Henderson's name and address.

2. **Click** in the left margin **beside "Ms. Diane Henderson."** The line will be highlighted.

3. **Press and hold** the **Shift key** and **click** in the left margin **next to the last line of the addres**s. All lines between the first and second clicks will be highlighted. (This is a quick way to select a series of paragraphs.)

4. **Click** on the **Copy button** in the toolbar.

In the next procedure, you will use the Go To command to get to page 2.

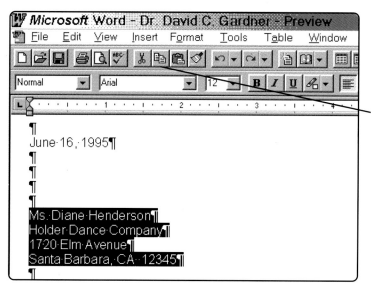

Using the Go To Command

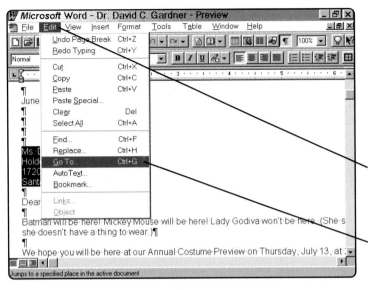

Using the Go To command is a quick way to move around in multipage documents. In this example you will use it to go to the top of page 2.

1. **Click** on **Edit** in the menu bar. A pull-down menu will appear.

2. **Click** on **Go To**. The Go To dialog box will appear.

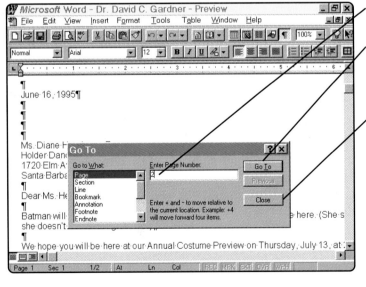

3. **Type** the **number 2**.

4. **Click** on **Go To**. The insertion point will move to the top of page 2.

5. **Click** on **Close**. The Go To box will disappear, and page 2 will be displayed on your screen.

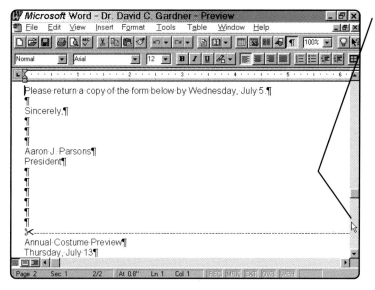

6. Click on the **scroll bar** about three quarters of the way down. This will take you three quarters of the way through the file and bring the return form into view.

Using the Paste Button

1. Place the **mouse pointer** to the **left** of the **para-graph symbol above "I will be attending." Click** to set your cursor in place.

2. Press Enter to insert another blank line in the text. You will now see three paragraph symbols above the sentence "I will be attending."

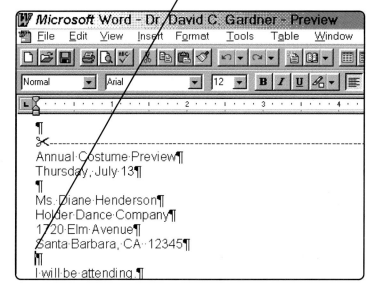

3. **Click** on the **Paste button** in the toolbar.

The text you copied to the Clipboard with the Copy tool is now pasted in the letter at the insertion point.

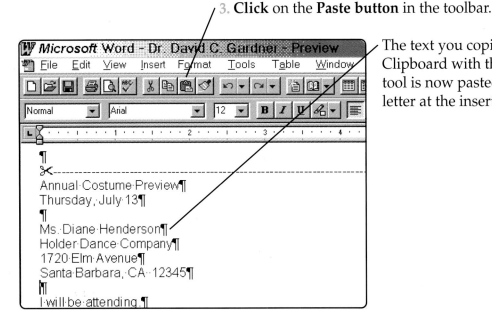

4. **Click** on the **Save button** in the toolbar to save your work.

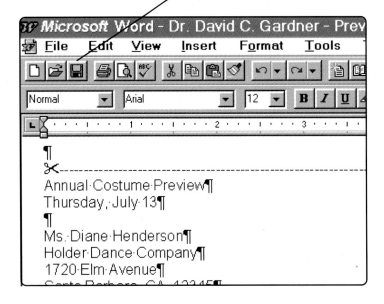

WORD FOR WINDOWS 95

**Part II: Formatting a Document
and Printing an Envelope and a Label**

Customizing Text

You will love the ease with which you can add special features to your text such as bold and italic type. You can further emphasize portions of text by changing the size of the font. You can center text and create a bulleted list at the click of your mouse. In this chapter, you will do the following:

- ✔ Change type size
- ✔ Convert text to UPPER CASE
- ✔ Make text **bold**, *italic*, and <u>underlined</u>
- ✔ Center text
- ✔ Make a bulleted list
- ✔ Highlight text

CHANGING TYPE SIZE

In this section you will increase the size of the type in the first line of the letter.

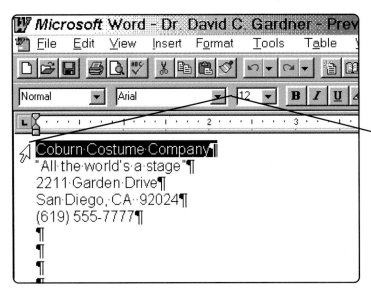

1. **Press and hold** the **Ctrl key** then **press Home** (Ctrl + Home) to go to the top of the file if you're not already there.

2. **Click** in the left margin **beside "Coburn Costume Company."** The line will be highlighted.

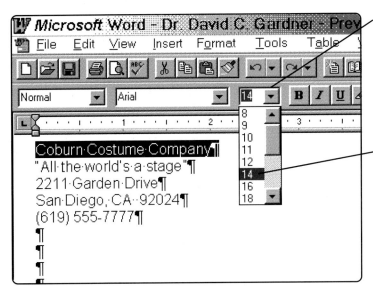

3. **Click** on ▼ to the right of the Font size box in the formatting toolbar. (On your screen the number 12 is in the box.) A pull-down menu will appear.

4. **Click** on **14**. The pull-down menu will disappear, and the highlighted (selected) text will appear in 14 point type.

CONVERTING TEXT TO UPPERCASE

Word 7 makes it easy to change the case of the letters you have already typed (i.e., make lower case letters all capitals.) You must first highlight the text you want to change. If you've been following along with the steps in this chapter, you've already highlighted "Coburn Costume Company."

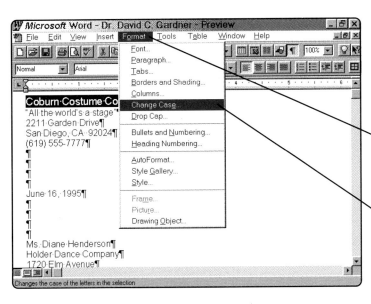

1. **Click** on **Format** in the menu bar. The Format menu will appear.

2. **Click** on **Change Case**. The Change Case dialog box will appear.

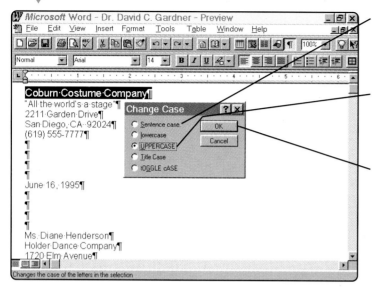

Notice that each of the names in the list shows you how that text will look.

3. **Click** on **UPPERCASE** to place a dot in the circle, if one isn't already there.

4. **Click** on **OK**. The dialog box will close and "Coburn Costume Company" will appear in capital letters.

MAKING TEXT BOLD

In this section you will make the type in "Coburn Costume Company" boldface.

1. **Click** on the **Bold button** (the large **B**) in the formatting toolbar. The selected text will appear in boldface type.

Notice that the Bold button appears pressed in. This tells you that the selected text is now bold. The Bold button works like a pushbutton. Once the text is selected, click on the Bold button to turn it on. Click on it again to turn it off.

MAKING TEXT ITALIC

In this section you will add italics to the quote in the letterhead address.

1. **Click** in the left margin **beside "All the world's a stage."** The line will be highlighted.

2. **Click** on the **Italics button** (the large slanted I) in the formatting toolbar. The selected text will appear in italics. Notice that the Italics button appears pressed in. The Italics button also works like a pushbutton.

UNDERLINING TEXT

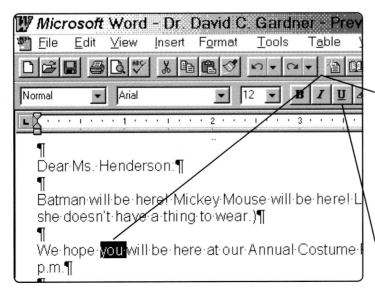

1. **Click** on the ▼ on the scroll bar until you can see the "We hope" sentence.

2. **Place** the **mouse pointer on top** of the word "**you**." The pointer will become an I-beam.

3. **Click twice** to highlight the word "you."

4. **Click** on the **Underline button** in the formatting toolbar.

CENTERING TEXT

In this section you will center all five lines at the top of the page. You can highlight all of the lines and apply the centering command to all five at the same time. You will then center two other portions of text in the letter.

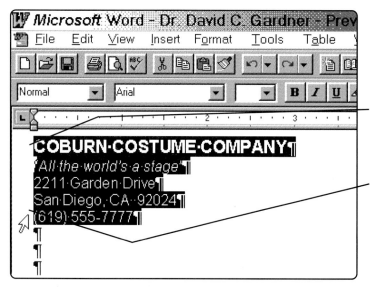

1. **Press and hold Ctrl** and **press Home** (Ctrl + Home) to get back to the beginning of the file.

2. **Click** in the left margin **beside "Coburn Costume Company"** to highlight it.

3. **Press and hold** the **Shift key** and **click** in the left margin **beside "(619) 555-7777."** All the lines between clicks will be highlighted.

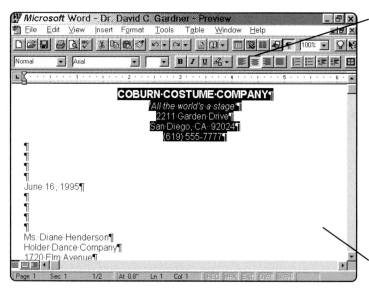

4. **Click** on the **Center button** in the formatting toolbar. The highlighted text will be centered across the page. Notice that the Center button appears pressed in and lighter in color. (The Center button does *not* work like a pushbutton. You have to click on another text alignment button to change the alignment.)

5. **Click anywhere** to remove the highlighting.

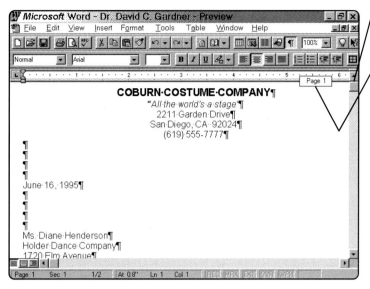

6. Press and hold on the **scroll button**.

Notice that a flag appears, showing that you are on page 1.

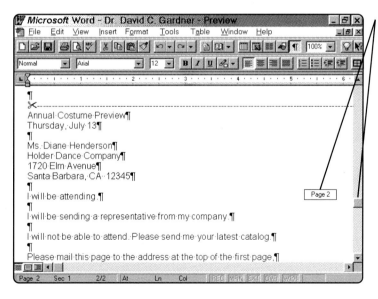

7. **Drag** the **scroll button** about two-thirds of the way down the scroll bar so that it looks like the one in this example. Notice that the flag now specifies page 2.

8. Click the **mouse pointer** in the left margin **beside "Annual Costume Preview"** to highlight it.

9. Press and **hold** the **Shift key** and **click** in the left margin **beside Thursday, July 13**. Both lines will be highlighted.

10. Click on the **Center button** in the formatting toolbar. Both lines will be centered within the page.

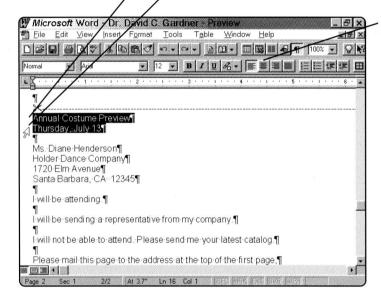

11. Click repeatedly on the ▼ on the scroll bar to go to the end of the letter.

12. Repeat steps 8 through 10 to center the last two lines of the letter.

13. Click on the **Save button** on the toolbar to save all your work.

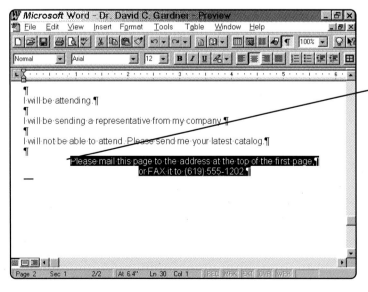

"READING" THE FORMATTING TOOLBAR

When you move the insertion point to the beginning of a paragraph, the settings in the formatting toolbar will reflect the formatting or styles in the paragraph. In this section you will see how the toolbar reflects the formatting of "Coburn Costume Company."

1. **Press and hold** the **Ctrl Key**. Then **press** the **Home key** (Ctrl + Home) to return to the top of the letter.

Notice the settings on the toolbar:

❖ Normal is the standard (default) style of all Word documents. This is the style used in the examples in this book.

❖ Arial and 14 points are the font and font size of this paragraph. If you select (highlight) a paragraph that has more than one font style and/or size, no settings will show in the boxes.

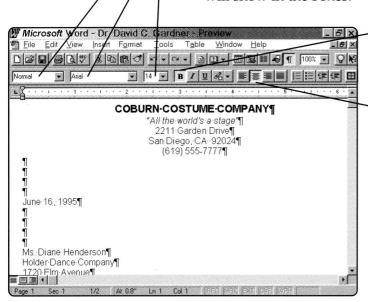

❖ The Bold button is pressed in. This shows that the paragraph is bold.

❖ The Center button is pressed in. This shows that the paragraph is centered across the page.

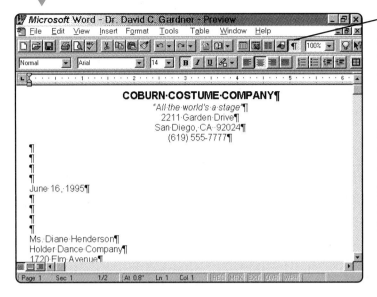

❖ When the Paragraph symbol on the standard toolbar is pressed in, the formatting marks show.

If your type ever behaves strangely, pay attention to these buttons. Chances are that you clicked on a button for one paragraph and forgot to click it off for the next paragraph.

MAKING A BULLETED LIST

In this section you will make four paragraphs into a list with bullets. It's as easy as clicking your mouse.

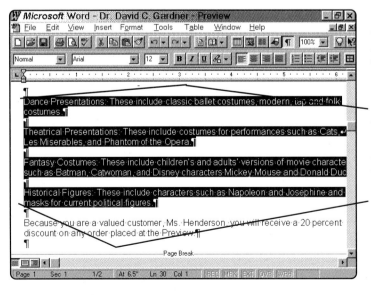

1. Click on the **scroll bar** until you can see the four paragraphs that describe the costumes.

2. Click in the left margin **beside "Dance Presentations."** The line will be highlighted.

3. Press and hold the **Shift key** as you **click** in the left margin **beside "masks..."** All the lines between clicks will be highlighted.

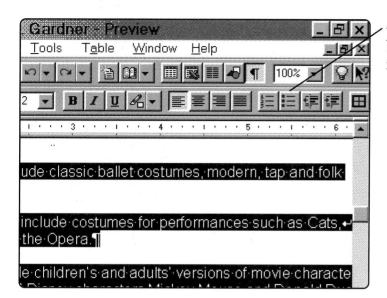

4. Click on the **Bullets button** on the right of the formatting toolbar.

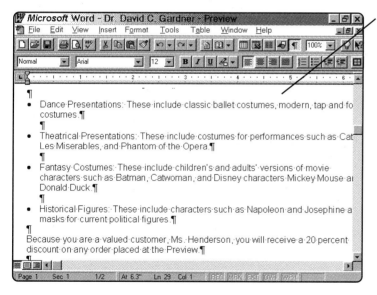

5. Click anywhere on the document to remove the highlighting so you can see the bulleted list.

Isn't that terrific?

CREATING A CUSTOMIZED BULLET

You can create a bullet using any character from any font you have. In this example, you'll use a check box from the Wingdings font to create a standard (default) bullet.

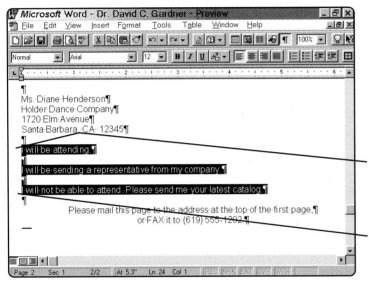

1. Click and hold on the **scroll button** and **drag** it three-quarters of the way down the scroll bar. You should be able to see the three reply sentences at the end of the letter.

2. Click in the left margin **beside "I will be attending."** to highlight the sentence.

3. Press and hold the **Shift key** and **click** in the left margin **beside "I will not be able to attend."** All three lines will be highlighted.

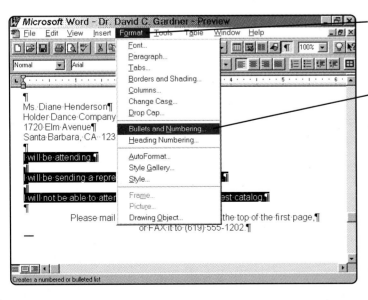

4. Click on **Format** in the menu bar. The Format menu will appear.

5. Click on **Bullets and Numbering**. The Bullets and Numbering dialog box will appear.

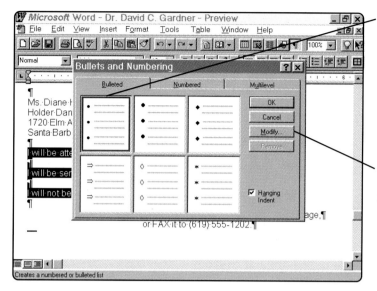

Notice that there is a border around the first bulleted list. This shows you that the "small dot" bullets are now selected as the standard (default) bullet in the selection list.

6. **Click** on **Modify**. The Modify Bulleted List dialog box will appear.

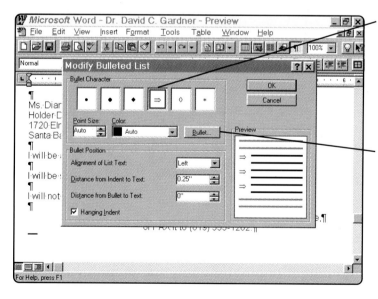

7. **Click** on the **bullet** you want to replace in the standard selection list. In this example, we'll replace the "open arrow" with a check box.

8. **Click** on **Bullet**. The Symbol dialog box will appear.

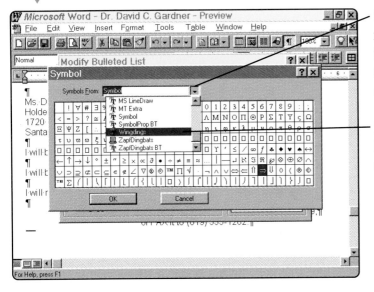

9. Click on the ▼ to the right of the Symbols From text box. A list of fonts will appear. (Your list may appear different.)

10. Click on **Wingdings** to highlight it. Wingdings will appear in the text box.

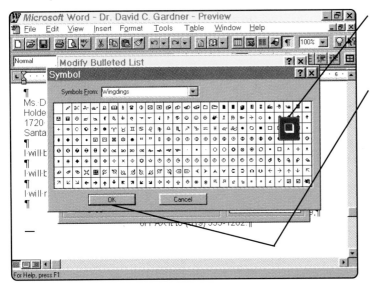

11. Click on the **check box** (third column from the right, third row down).

12. Click on **OK**. The Symbol dialog box will close.

Notice that the check box has replaced the "open arrow" in the bullet character list.

Notice also that the standard (default) indent from the bullet to the text is set at .25 inches.

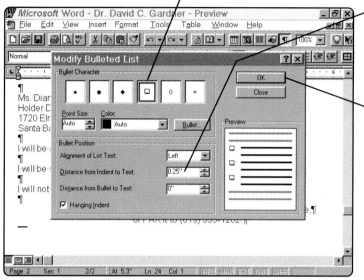

13. **Click** on **OK**. The dialog box will close, and the highlighted paragraphs will appear with check boxes.

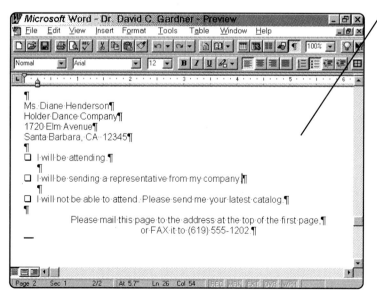

14. **Click anywhere** on the document to remove the highlighting from the sentences.

REMOVING BULLETS

In this example you will remove the last check box on page 2.

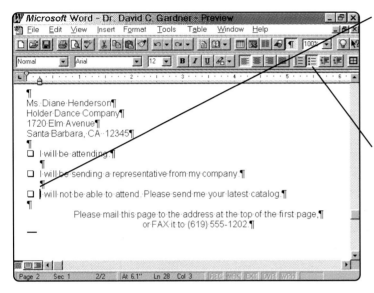

1. **Click** to the **left** of **"I will not"** in the last sentence with a check box. (Notice that you cannot place the cursor to the left of the check box.)

2. **Click** on the **Bullets button** on the formatting toolbar. The bullet will disappear.

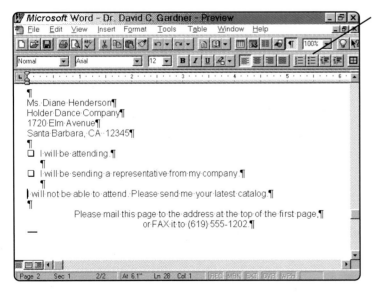

3. **Click** on the **Bullets button** again to put the check box back in the sentence.

HIGHLIGHTING TEXT WITH COLOR

The highlighting tool gives you several colors to choose from that look great when used in an electronic file, such as e-mail. However, if you're going to print your document on a regular laser printer, remember that the highlighting will print as a shade of gray.

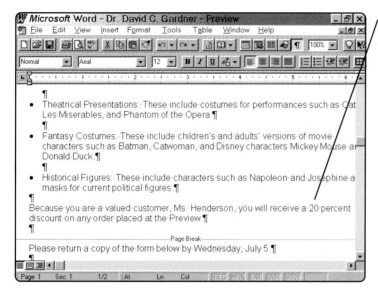

1. **Click repeatedly** on the ▲ on the scroll bar to see the "20 percent" sentence before the page break.

Changing the Highlight Color

The first step in this section will change the highlight color.

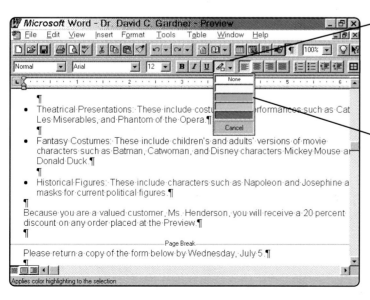

1. **Click** on the ▼ to the right of the highlight button. A pull-down menu of colors will appear as you see in this example.

2. **Click** on the **green bar** in the menu. The menu will close, and the small square in the highlight button will become green.

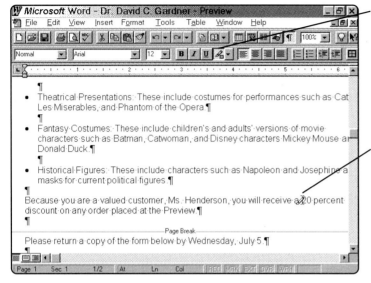

Notice that the highlight button looks pressed in and is active.

Applying Highlight Color

1. Click to **place** your cursor to the **left** of **"20 percent."**

Notice that your cursor has changed into an I-beam with a highlight pen.

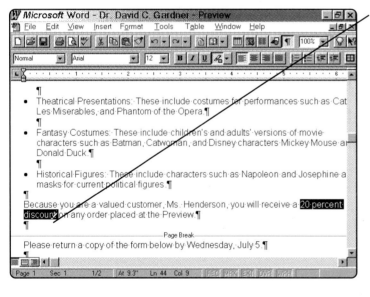

2. Press and hold the **mouse button** as you **drag** the cursor to the right and down one line to highlight "20 percent discount."

3. Release the **mouse button.** "20 percent discount" will be highlighted in green.

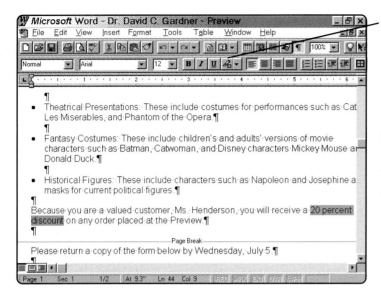

4. Click on the **highlight button** on the toolbar to turn off the highlighting function.

Note: This is an important step. If you forget to turn off the highlight button, the next time you highlight text for *any* reason, it will be highlighted with green.

REMOVING THE HIGHLIGHTING

If you're following along with the examples in this book, you could simply click on the Undo button on the standard toolbar to remove the highlighting. However, in this example, you'll learn how to remove the highlighting using the highlight button.

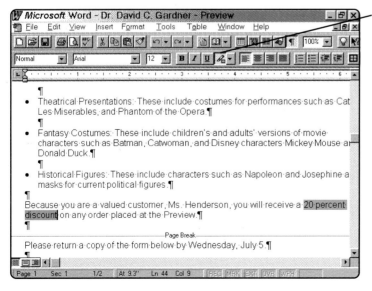

1. Click on the **highlight button** on the formatting toolbar. The button will look pressed in.

Notice that the small square in the button is green.

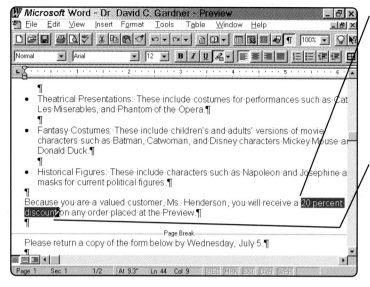

2. **Click** to **place** your cursor to the **left** of **"20 percent."**

Notice that your cursor has changed into an I-beam with a highlight pen.

3. **Press and hold** the **mouse button** as you **drag** the cursor to the right and down one line to highlight "20 percent discount."

4. **Release** the **mouse button**. The green highlighting will be removed.

5. **Click** on the **Undo button** on the standard toolbar to replace the green highlighting.

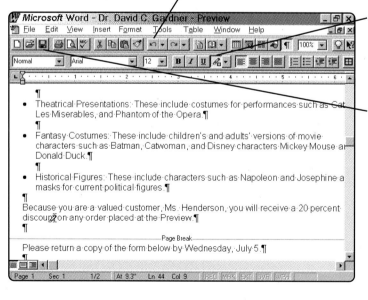

6. **Click** on the **highlight button** on the toolbar to turn off the highlighting command.

7. **Click** on the **Save button** to save your work.

Adding a Picture, a Shaded Border and Drawing a Line

You can easily create exciting visual effects in Word 7. There are some wonderful clip art pictures you can use to add interest to your documents. You can put a border around text and then add shading inside the border. Word also has a drawing program. In this chapter, you will do the following:

✔ Insert clip art into a document
✔ Draw a line with the drawing toolbar
✔ Put a border around text
✔ Add shading inside the border

WORKING WITH CLIP ART

In this section you will select a picture (a piece of clip art) from the Clip Art directory in Word and insert it into a document.

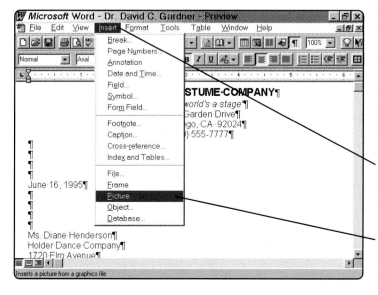

1. Press and hold the **Ctrl key** and **press** the **Home key** (Ctrl + Home) to go to the top of the file. In this example, it's important that your cursor be at the beginning of the file.

2. Click on **Insert** in the menu bar. The Insert menu will appear.

3. Click on **Picture**. The Insert Picture dialog box will appear.

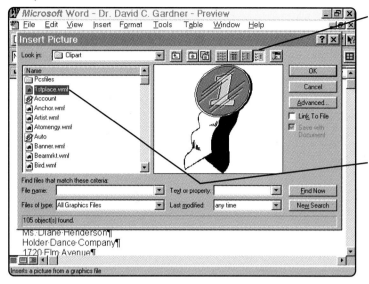

4. Click on the **Preview button**, if necessary. The Insert Picture dialog box will change to the preview file mode so that you can view files before you open them.

Notice that 1stplace.wmf is highlighted in the Name list. The 1stplace.wmf picture can be seen in the preview box to the right of the list.

5. Click repeatedly on the ▼ on the scroll bar to scroll down the list of pictures.

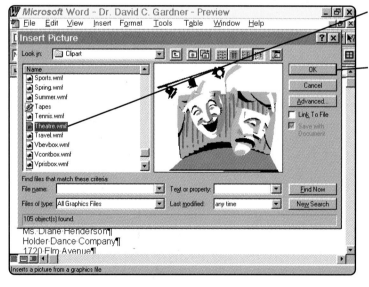

6. Click on **Theatre.wmf** to highlight it.

7. Click on **OK**. The dialog box will close, and the picture will appear in your letter at the cursor position.

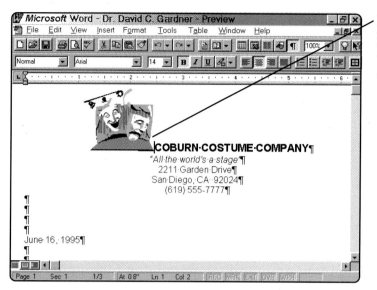

Notice that the graphic is inserted ahead of the text. In the next section you'll fix that.

INSERTING A FRAME

When you insert a graphic (piece of clip art) into a document, it is considered a separate line and displaces the text where it is placed. In this section you will put a frame around the graphic. This will cause the text to wrap (move) to the right of the graphic.

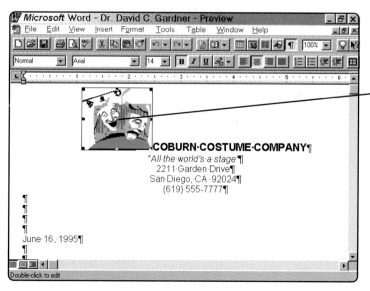

1. Click on the **graphic**. It will be surrounded by a selection border. A selection border has eight little squares, or handles, on its perimeter and is used to resize a graphic.

2. **Click** on **Insert** in the menu bar. The Insert menu will appear.

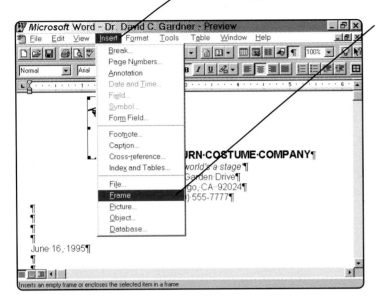

3. **Click** on **Frame**. A Microsoft Word message box will appear.

4. **Click** on **Yes** to switch to Page Layout View. This is a view that shows the placement of the graphic in relation to the text as it will be on the printed page. However, Page Layout View is slower for editing and scrolling.

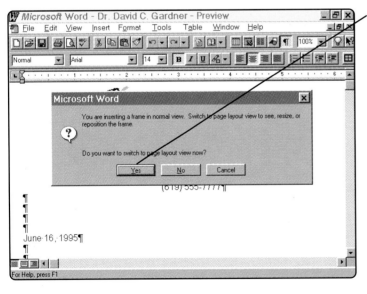

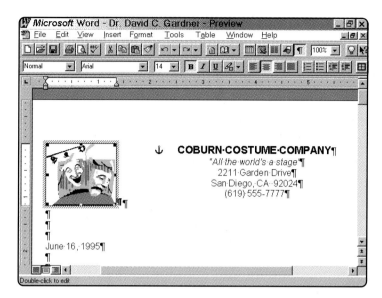

While the graphic is surrounded by the frame and selection border you can click and hold on the graphic and move it around the page. See Chapter 20, "Making a Customized Template," for more information on sizing and moving clip art.

DRAWING A LINE

In this section you will use Word's drawing program. Because drawn objects are not visible in the Normal View you should be in the Page Layout View. If you have been following along with this chapter, you are already in Page Layout View.

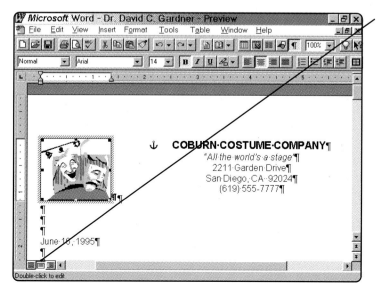

1. **Click** on the **Page Layout View button** at the bottom of your screen if you are not already in Page Layout View. It will look pressed in and lighter in color.

Opening the Drawing Toolbar

Word has a special toolbar for the drawing program.

1. Click on the **Drawing button** on the standard toolbar. The drawing toolbar will appear on your screen.

Selecting the Line

Now that the drawing toolbar is open, you need to tell Word what kind of line you want to draw. In this example you will select a single line with a shadow.

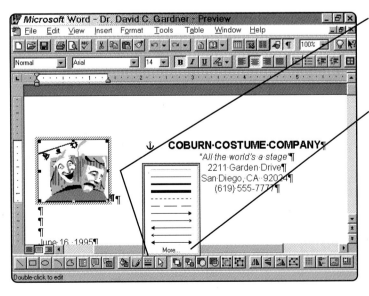

1. Click on the **Line Style button** on the drawing toolbar. A pop-up box of line styles will appear.

2. Click on **More** to see the Drawing Defaults dialog box.

Notice that the Weight shows .75 pt., which is a thin line. (In this book, the line that points to Weight is a 1 point line.)

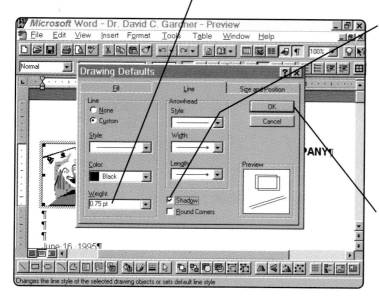

3. **Click** on **Shadow** to insert a ✔ in the box. (This will stay selected until you change it. So the next time you draw a line it will have a shadow unless you click on this box again to remove the ✔ before you draw the line.)

4. **Click** on **OK** to close the dialog box.

5. **Click** on the **Line tool** on the toolbar. The cursor will be in the shape of a plus sign (+).

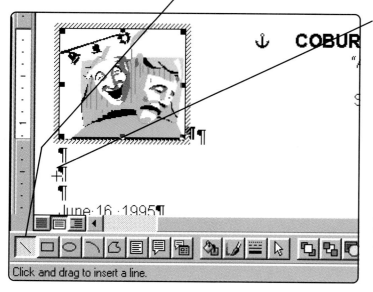

6. **Position** the **cursor** so that its center is at the spot where you want the line to begin. In this example, it's two lines above the date.

Be careful not to click the mouse button until you have positioned the plus sign (+). Extra clicks turn off the line function. If this happens, repeat steps 5 and 6.

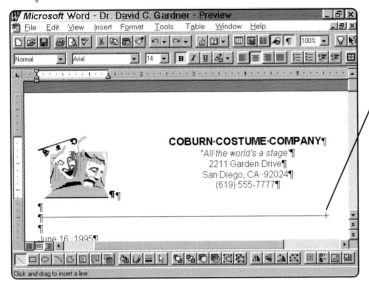

7. Press and hold the **Shift key.** This will force the line to be straight as you draw the line.

8. Press and hold the **mouse button** and **drag** the cursor across the page.

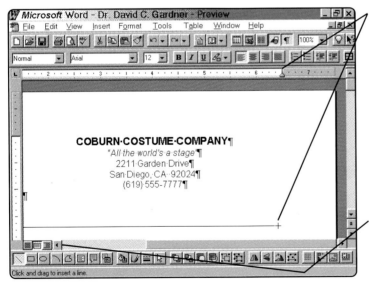

9. Drag the **line** to the **right,** *past* the edge of the screen. The window will jump over to give you a view of the right margin. **Release** the **mouse button** when the end of the line is at the 6.5 inch mark. You will see a thin line with a second shadow line underneath it.

10. Click repeatedly on the ◀ on the bottom scroll bar to bring the left margin back into view.

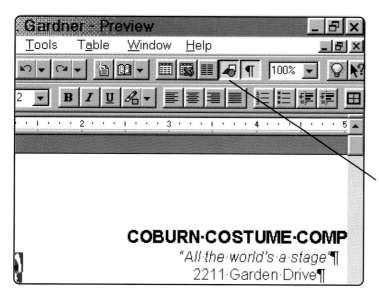

Removing the Drawing Toolbar

You won't need the drawing toolbar for the next section, so remove it from your screen.

1. Click on the **Drawing button** in the standard toolbar. The drawing toolbar will disappear.

CHANGING THE ALIGNMENT OF THE PICTURE

1. Click on the **Normal View button** at the bottom of the screen. The screen will return to the Normal View.

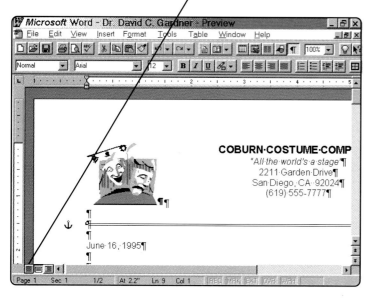

Remember, you can't see drawn objects in Normal View, so you won't see the line you drew. Also, the picture appears in a different place than you see in Page Layout View. This is because the picture has taken on the center alignment of the text. In this example, you will change the alignment of the picture to left alignment.

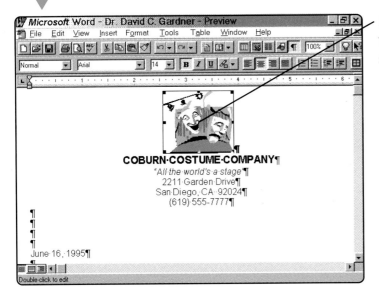

2. **Click** on the **picture**. It will be surrounded by a selection border.

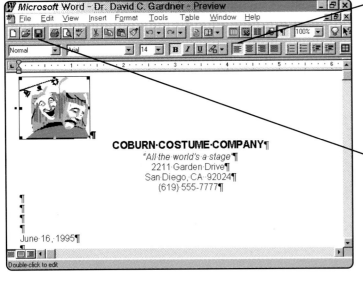

3. **Click** on the **Left-alignment button**. The picture will move to the left.

Here's your chance to see what the letter looks like in print.

4. **Click** on the **Save button** to save your work.

5. **Click** on the **Print button** to print the letter.

ADDING A SHADED BORDER AROUND TEXT

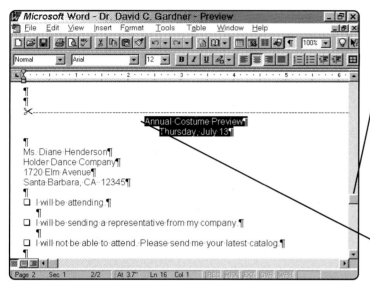

In this section you'll add a shaded border around the heading on the reply form on page 2.

1. **Press and hold** on the **scroll button** and **drag** it to page 2, two-thirds of the way down the scroll bar. You should be able to see the scissors.

2. **Click** to the **left** of "**Annual Costume Preview**" to highlight the line.

3. **Press and hold** the **Shift key** and **click** to the **left** of "**Thursday, July 13.**" Both lines will be highlighted.

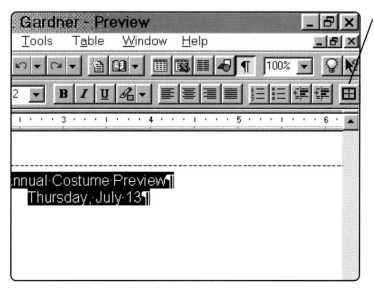

4. **Click** on the **Borders button** on the far right of the formatting toolbar. The borders toolbar will appear on your screen.

5. **Click** on the **Outside Border button**. A border that is 3/4 pt. wide will appear around the highlighted text. (Notice the 3/4 pt. indicator on the left of the toolbar.)

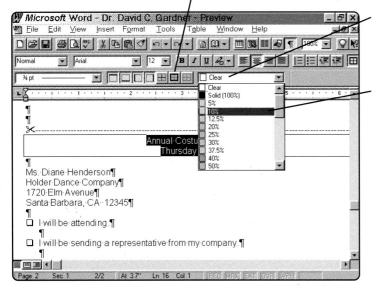

6. **Click** on the **Shading text box** on the toolbar. A pull-down list will appear.

7. **Click** on **10%**. The pull-down menu will disappear, and the border will appear with a light 10% shading.

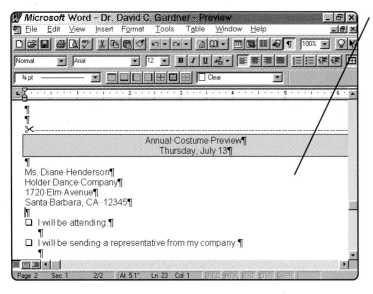

8. **Click anywhere** on the document to remove the highlighting and see the shaded border.

REMOVING A SHADED BORDER

To remove a shaded border, you must first highlight the text inside the border.

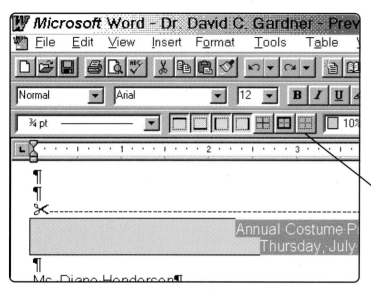

1. Click to the **left** of **"Annual Costume Preview"** to highlight the line.

2. Press and hold the **Shift key** and **click** to the **left** of the date line to highlight both lines.

3. Click on the **No Border button** on the toolbar to remove the border.

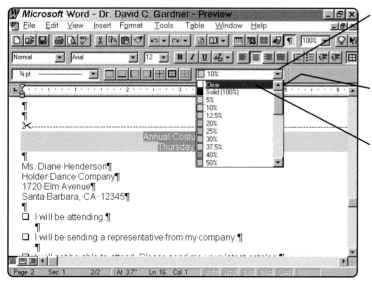

4. Click on the ▼ to the right of the Shading box. A pull-down list will appear.

5. Click on the ▲ to scroll up to Clear.

6. Click on **Clear**. The Shading will be removed.

UNDOING TWO PREVIOUS STEPS

You can reverse the last two steps you took to remove the border and the shading.

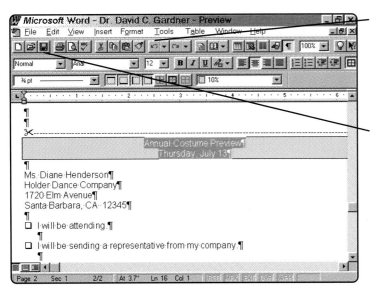

1. **Click two times** on the **Undo button**. The first click will replace the shading, and the second click will replace the outside border.

2. **Click** on the **Save button** to save your work.

REMOVING THE BORDER TOOLBAR

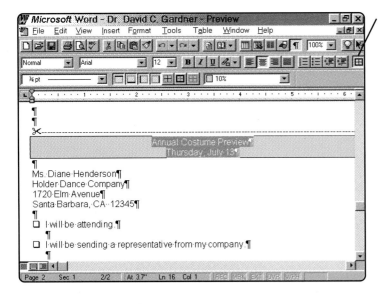

1. **Click** on the **Borders button** to remove the border toolbar from your screen.

Setting and Applying Tabs

Word 7 for Windows 95 has tabs preset at every half inch. To insert a tab, simply press the Tab key. You can also set your own tabs. When you set a tab, the preset tabs between the new tab and the left margin disappear. In this chapter, you will set and apply the following kinds of tabs:

✔ The standard left-aligned tab that lines words up on the first letter: Josh

  Jessica

✔ A leader (line) that ends at a right-aligned tab: Josh _____

    Jessica ___

✔ A right-aligned tab that aligns words on the last letter: Josh

    Jessica

✔ A center-aligned tab that centers words: Josh

    Jessica

✔ A tab that aligns numbers on the decimal point: 9.50

    99.50

GETTING READY TO SET TABS

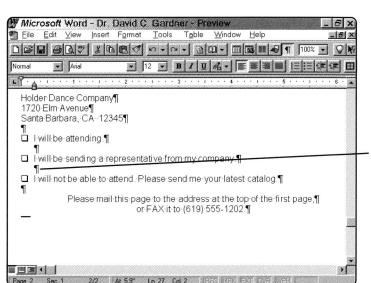

1. **Click** on the **scroll bar** to go to the end of the Preview letter if you are not already there. You should be able to see the three check boxes at the end of the letter.

2. **Click** on the **blank line** above the last check box.

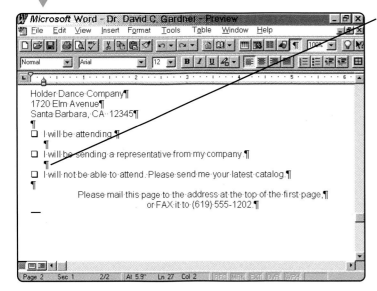

Notice that the paragraph symbol is indented to align with the typed sentence. This is because these three sentences have been formatted as a bulleted list and the bulleted list feature is set to have a .25-inch indent.

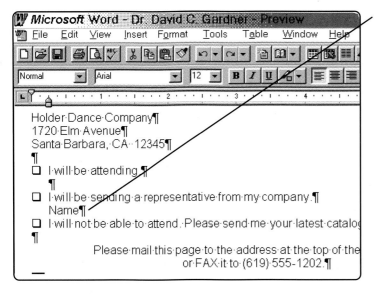

3. **Type Name**. Notice that the paragraph mark moves as you type.

INSERTING A LEADER WITH A RIGHT-ALIGNED TAB

A common example of a leader is the dotted line in a table of contents that connects a chapter and its page number, as shown here:

Chapter 2 34

Another common example of a leader is the fill-in-the-blank solid line seen on forms, for example:

Name _____

To create these kinds of leaders, use the Right-Aligned Tab button.

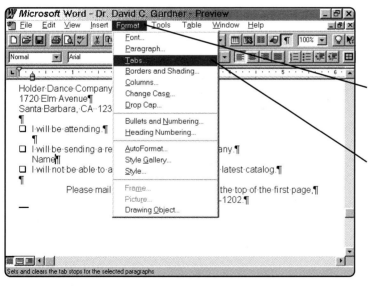

In this section you will insert a solid line after "Name."

1. **Click** on **Format** in the menu bar. The Format menu will appear.

2. **Click** on **Tabs**. The Tabs dialog box will appear.

3. **Type 4** to set a tab stop at 4 inches.

4. **Click** on **Right** to put a dot in the circle.

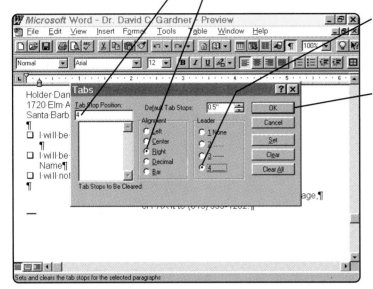

5. **Click** on **4** (the solid line option) to insert a dot in the circle.

6. **Click** on **OK**. The dialog box will close, and a right-aligned tab mark will appear in the ruler at 4 inches.

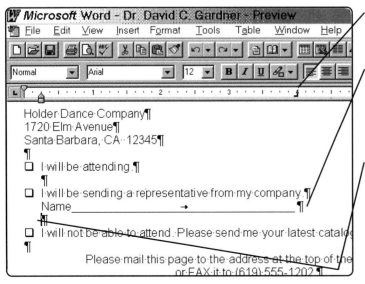

Notice the right-aligned tab mark at 4 inches.

7. **Press** the **Tab key**. The paragraph mark will move to the 4-inch mark and a line will appear in the text.

8. **Press** the **Enter key** to move the cursor to the next line.

SOME NOTES ABOUT TABS

Note 1: When you set a tab in an already-typed document, the tab applies *only* to the paragraph in which you set it. In this example, you added a second line to the paragraph that contains the tab by pressing the Enter key at the end of the line. Therefore, the tab that you set at 4 inches still applies to this new line. It does not, however, apply to any other paragraph. If you want a tab to apply to more than one paragraph, highlight all appropriate paragraphs before you set the tab.

Note 2: When you set a tab, it erases all preset tabs between it and the left margin. In the previous example, the tab you set at 4 inches erased the preset tabs up to the 4 inch point. In this next example, you will set a new left-aligned tab .5 inch from the left margin.

SETTING A LEFT-ALIGNED TAB

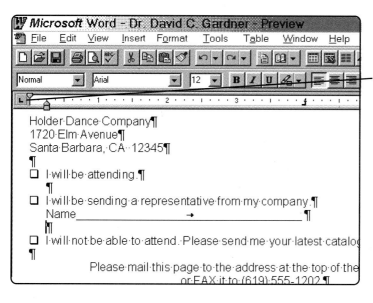

You can use the mouse to set a tab directly in the ruler.

1. **Confirm** that the left-aligned tab mark appears on the tab button on the ruler.

2. Place the **mouse pointer** in the ruler (it will become an arrow) so that the arrow points at, but is not on top of, the **.5-inch mark** on the ruler.

3. Click the **mouse button**. A left-aligned tab mark will appear just below the .5-inch mark on the ruler line. If the tab mark does not appear, you probably placed the arrow on top of the .5-inch mark. Try again.

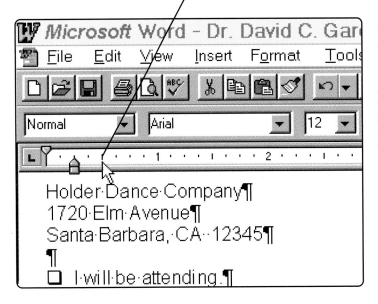

4. Press the **Tab key** and **type Title**.

5. Press the **Tab key** to insert a solid line.

6. Press Enter to move the cursor to the next line.

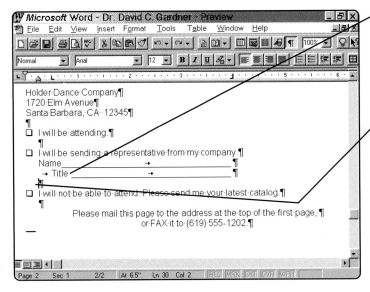

CLEARING A TAB

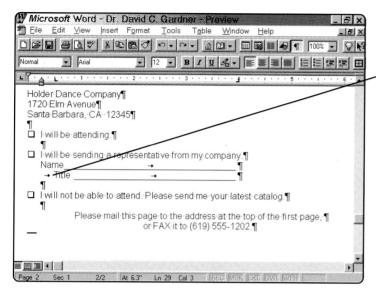

You'll love how easy it is to clear a tab.

1. Click to the **left** of **"Title"** to place the cursor.

2. Press the **Backspace key.** "Title" will backspace one tab position and be aligned under "Name." Notice the leader line extends to fill the space.

Now you will clear the tab you set at .5 inch.

3. Place the arrow on **top** of the **left-aligned tab mark** and **press and hold** the **mouse button.** You will see a dotted line in the document at the tab position.

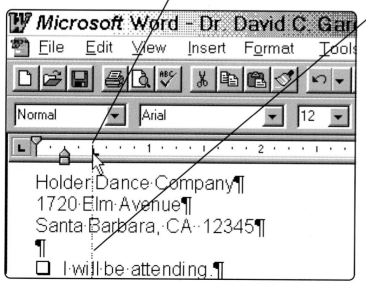

4. Continue to **press and hold** the **mouse button** and **drag** the tab mark down into the document.

5. Release the **mouse button.** The tab will be removed from the ruler. Isn't this a really cool feature?

6. Press and hold the **Ctrl key** then **type** the letter **s** (Ctrl + s). This is another way to save your work.

OPENING A NEW DOCUMENT

In the remaining sections of this chapter, you'll learn how to set a right-aligned tab and a center-aligned tab with the mouse, and set a decimal tab with the mouse and from the menu bar. Since the tabs will not be used in Preview, you will open a new document. You don't need to close Preview in order to open a new document. Word allows multiple documents to be open at the same time.

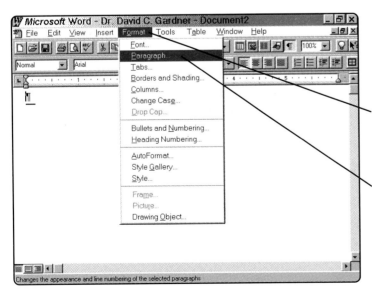

1. **Click** on the **New Document button** on the toolbar. A new document will appear on your screen on top of Preview.

CHANGING LINE SPACING

In this section you'll change the line spacing from single to double for the entire document.

1. **Click** on **Format** on the menu bar. The Format menu will appear.

2. **Click** on **Paragraph**. The Paragraph dialog box will appear.

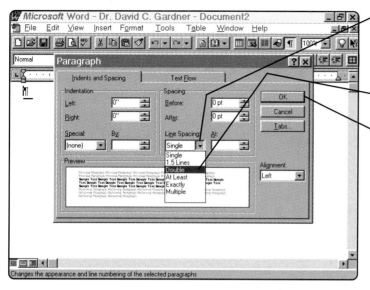

3. Click on the ▼ to the right of Single. A pull-down list will appear.

4. Click on **Double**.

5. Click on **OK**. The dialog box will close. You are now set to type with double spacing. When you press Enter, the cursor will automatically go down two lines.

SETTING A RIGHT-ALIGNED TAB

Tabs set at the beginning of a new document will apply to the entire document.

1. Click two times on the **Tab button** on the ruler to change the setting from the left-aligned tab symbol to the right-aligned tab symbol you see in this example.

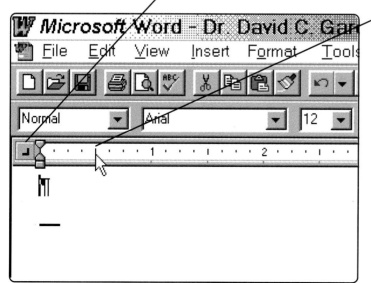

2. Place the **mouse pointer** in the lower half of the ruler at the **.5-inch mark**. It will become an arrow.

3. Click to insert a right-aligned tab at this position. (If the tab mark does not appear, you probably placed the arrow on top of the line. Move the arrow slightly and try again.)

SETTING A CENTER-ALIGNED TAB

In this section you will use the mouse to set a center-aligned tab at the 2-inch mark.

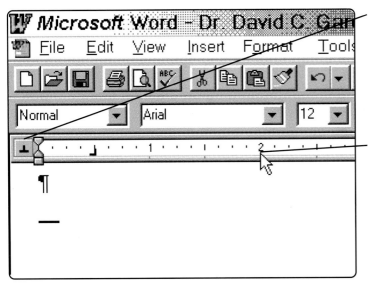

1. **Click three times** on the **Tab button** on the ruler to change the setting from the right-aligned symbol to the center-aligned symbol you see in this example.

2. **Place** the **mouse pointer** in the lower half of the ruler at the **2-inch mark**. Do not let the arrow touch the 2-inch mark.

3. **Click** to set the center-aligned tab in place.

You will use this tab setting later in this chapter in the section "Applying Tabs."

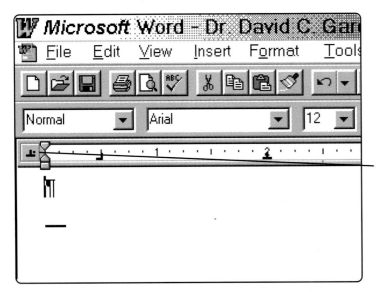

SETTING A DECIMAL TAB

In this section you will use the mouse to set a decimal tab at 3.5 inches.

1. **Click two times** on the **Tab button** to change the setting from the center-aligned symbol to the decimal symbol you see in this example.

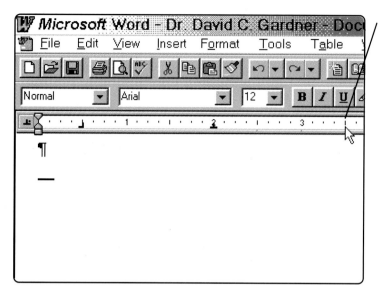

2. Place the **mouse pointer** in the lower half of the ruler at the **3.5-inch mar**k. Do not let the arrow touch the vertical mark.

3. Click to set the decimal tab in place.

You will use this tab setting later in the chapter in the section "Applying Tabs."

In this next section you will use the tab set dialog box to set a second decimal tab.

4. Click on **Format** in the menu bar. The Format menu will appear.

5. Click on **Tabs**. The Tabs dialog box will appear.

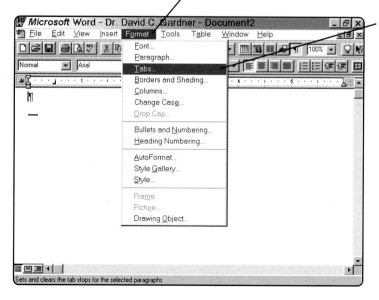

Notice that the tabs you set with the mouse are listed in the Tab Stop Position list box.

6. **Type 5**. It will replace the highlighted 0.5" in the Tab Stop Position box.

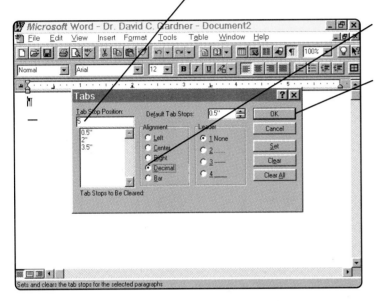

7. **Click** on **Decimal** to place a dot in the circle.

8. **Click** on **OK** to set the tab and close the dialog box.

APPLYING TABS

In this section you will apply the tabs you set in the previous sections. Because you set the tabs at the beginning of a blank document, they will apply from this point on until you reset them. As you type, notice how each text entry aligns on the tab stop in the ruler.

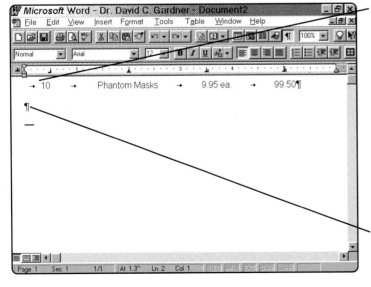

1. **Press Tab** and **type 10**.

2. **Press Tab** and **type Phantom Masks**. Notice that the text moves to the left as you type.

3. **Press Tab** and type **9.95 ea.**

4. **Press Tab** and **type 99.50**.

5. **Press Enter**. The cursor will move down two lines.

6. **Press Tab** and **type 5**. Notice the "5" is right-aligned under "10."

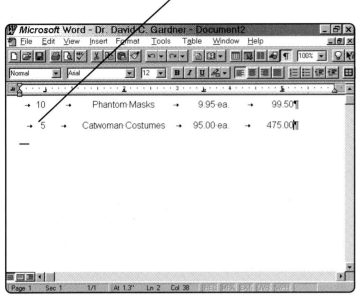

7. **Press Tab** and **type Catwoman Costumes**. Notice that it is centered under the entry above it.

8. **Press Tab** and type **95.00 ea.** Notice that the decimal points are lined up.

9. **Press Tab** and **type 475.00**. Again, notice that the decimal points are lined up.

SWITCHING BETWEEN OPEN DOCUMENTS

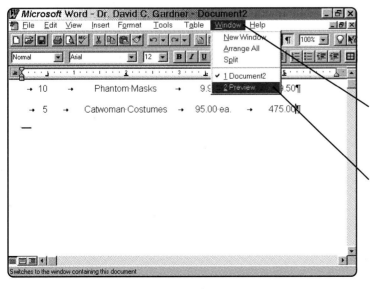

In this section you will switch back and forth between the unnamed file on your screen and Preview.

1. **Click** on **Window** in the menu bar. The Window menu will appear.

2. **Click** on **Preview**. The Preview file will appear on your screen exactly where you were when you opened the new document.

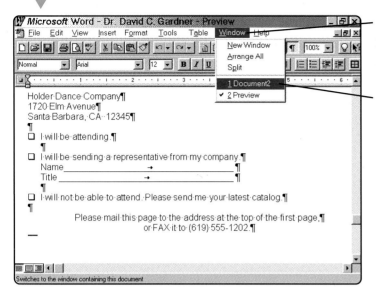

3. Click on **Window** in the menu bar. The Window menu will appear.

4. Click on **Document2** to return to the tab document.

CLOSING WITHOUT SAVING

Because this exercise was meant only as practice in setting different types of tabs and will not be used later in the book, you don't need to save the document.

1. Click on **File** in the menu bar. A pull-down menu will appear.

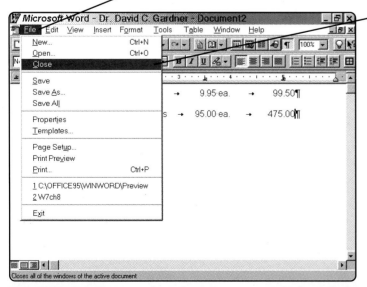

2. Click on **Close**. Because you haven't saved this document, you will see a Microsoft Word dialog box asking if you want to save the document.

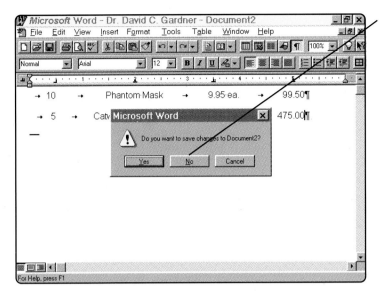

3. **Click** on **No**. The document will close without being saved. You will see Preview on your screen. It will be exactly as you left it when you opened the new document.

Adding a Section Divider, Header, and Page Number

In Word 7 for Windows you can divide a document into sections and format each section separately, allowing you to make elements like margins, headers, and footers different in each section. A *header* is information that is printed at the top of the page. For example, in this book the page number and book title is a header on every left page and the chapter title and page number is a header on every right page. In this chapter, you will do the following:

✔ Make page 2 of the sample Preview file into a separate section and change the top margin
✔ Insert a header on page 2 of the sample document
✔ Insert a page number on page 2

SEPARATING A DOCUMENT INTO TWO SECTIONS

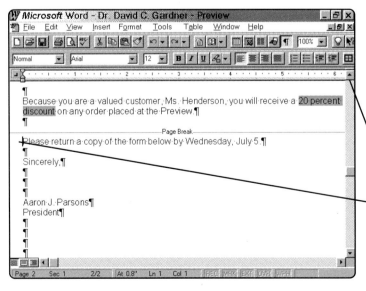

In this section you will change the top margin on page 2. To do this you will make page 2 a separate section.

1. **Click** on ▲ to scroll up so that you can see the end of page 1.

2. **Click** to the **left** of **"Please return"** at the top of page 2.

3. **Click** on **File** in the menu bar. The File menu will appear.

4. **Click** on **Page Setup**. The Page Setup dialog box will appear.

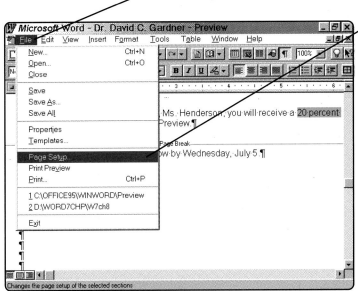

5. **Click** on the **Margins tab** if it's not already the front tab in the dialog box.

6. **Click twice** on the ▲ to the right of the Top margin box to change it to 1".

7. **Click** on the ▼ to the right of the Apply To box. A pull-down list will appear.

8. **Click** on **This Point Forward** to change the margin for page 2.

9. **Click** on **OK**. The dialog box will close.

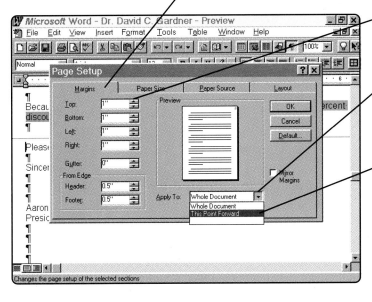

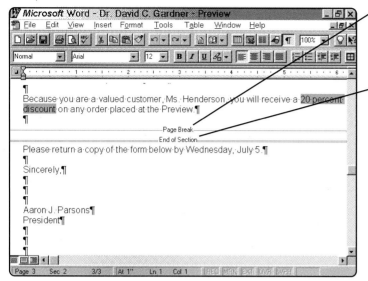

Notice that the Page Break is still there. You will delete it in the next section.

Notice the double line indicating the end of Section 1 (and the start of the new section.)

Note: Be sure to complete the next section or you'll end up with three pages in your document.

Deleting the Page Break

1. **Place** the **mouse pointer** in the left margin **on top** of the **Page Break line**. The pointer will change to a right-facing arrow.

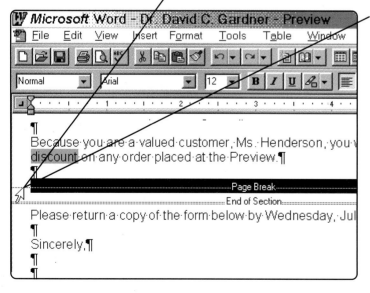

2. **Click** on the **Page Break line**. The Page Break line will be highlighted.

3. **Press** the **Delete key** on your keyboard. The Page Break line will disappear. The double line indicating the new section will still be there.

CREATING A HEADER

When you create a header in Word, it will appear at the top of every page of the document unless you tell Word otherwise.

1. **Click** at the **bottom of page 1** to place the cursor.

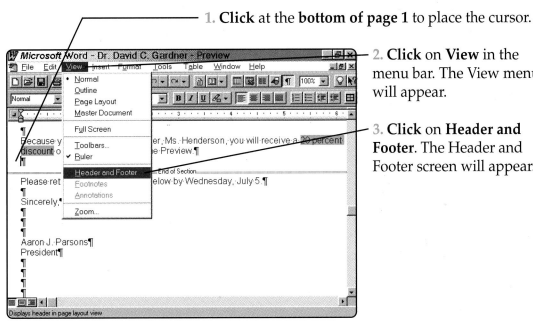

2. **Click** on **View** in the menu bar. The View menu will appear.

3. **Click** on **Header and Footer**. The Header and Footer screen will appear.

Notice the following:

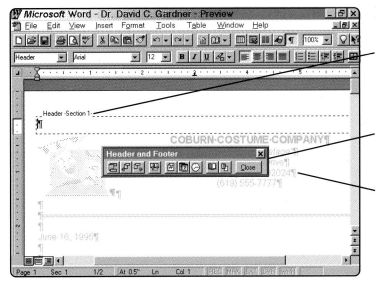

❖ The Header-Section 1 box with the cursor automatically placed in the box

❖ The Header and Footer toolbar

❖ The grayed-out document in the background

4. **Type Ms. Diane Henderson** and **press Enter**. The header box will expand.

5. **Click** on the **Date button** on the toolbar. Today's date will be inserted into the Header box.

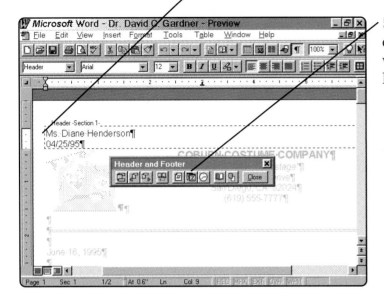

PRINTING THE HEADER ON PAGE TWO ONLY

Now you have to go to Page Setup and tell Word to print the header on page 2 only.

1. **Click** on the **Page Setup button** on the toolbar. The Page Setup dialog box will appear.

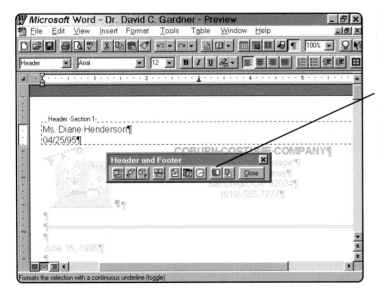

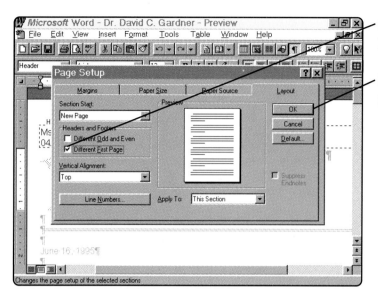

2. **Click** on **Different First Page** to put a ✔ in the box.

3. **Click** on **OK**. The Page Setup dialog box will close.

Notice that the box labeled "First Page Header-Section 1" is now empty. You can see a grayed-out page 1 in the background.

4. **Click** on the **Show Next button** on the Header and Footer toolbar to move to page 2.

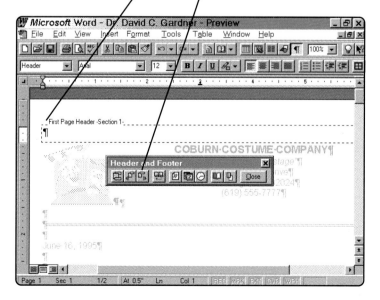

Notice that the header is now labeled "Header-Section 2," and the text you typed is in the box. You can see a grayed-out page 2 in the background.

CHANGING THE DISTANCE BETWEEN THE HEADER AND THE DOCUMENT TEXT

You can use your mouse to increase the distance between the header and the document text.

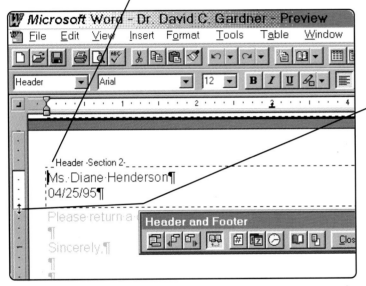

1. **Place** the **mouse pointer** on the **bottom margin boundary** on the vertical ruler. It will change to a double-headed arrow.

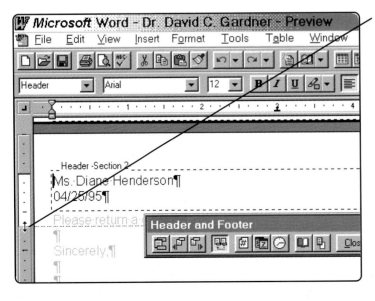

2. **Press and hold** the **mouse button** and **drag** the boundary down to **below** the grayed-out "**Please return**" line. **Release** the **mouse button**.

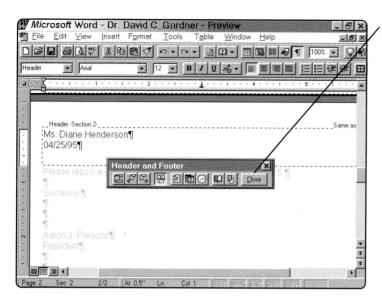

3. **Click** on **Close** in the Header and Footer toolbar.

Although the header will print, you will not see it in the Normal View. Later in the chapter, you will change the view.

ADDING A PAGE NUMBER

You can add page numbers from any point in the document, but to follow this example you should be on page 1.

1. **Click anywhere** on page 1 if your cursor is not already there.

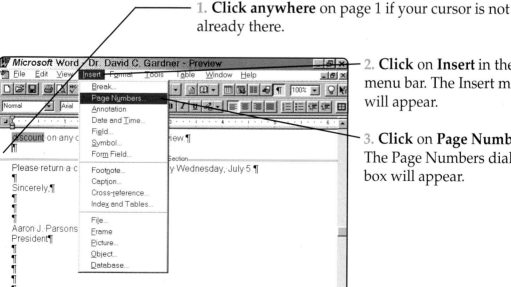

2. **Click** on **Insert** in the menu bar. The Insert menu will appear.

3. **Click** on **Page Numbers.** The Page Numbers dialog box will appear.

4. **Confirm** that **Bottom of Page (Footer)** is in the Position box.

5. **Click** on **Show Number on First Page** to *remove* the ✔ from the box, if necessary.

6. **Click** on the ▼ to the right of the Alignment box. A pull-down list will appear.

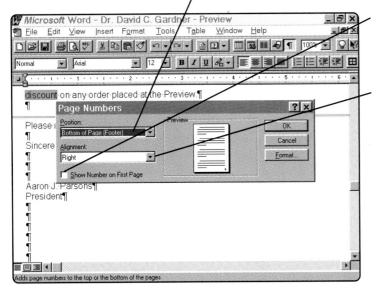

7. **Click** on **Center**. The pull-down list will disappear, and Center will now be in the Alignment box.

8. **Click** on **OK**. The Page Number dialog box will close, and you will be returned to your Normal View screen. You cannot see the page number in the Normal View.

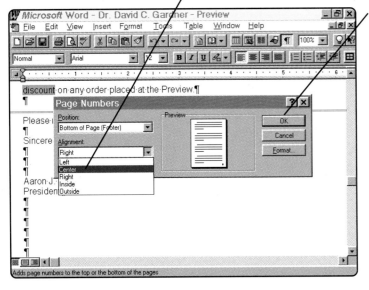

VIEWING THE HEADER AND PAGE NUMBER

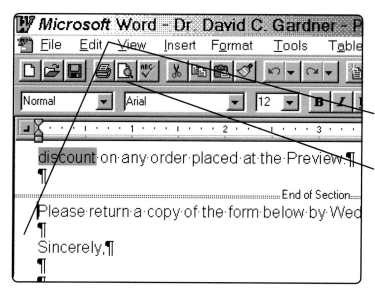

Print Preview is one of the views in which you can see the header and page number.

1. **Click anywhere** on Page 2.

2. **Click** on the **Print Preview button** on the standard toolbar.

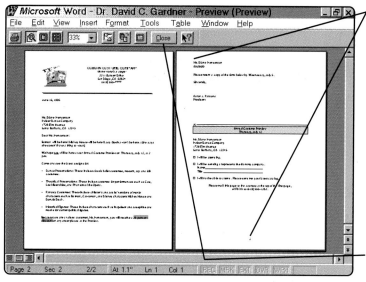

Notice the header at the top of page 2 and the page number at the bottom of page 2.

If you want to zoom in to see the header, position the magnifying glass over the header and press your mouse button. Then press your mouse button again to zoom out.

3. **Click** on **Close** to return to the Normal View.

4. **Press and hold** the **Ctrl key** on your keyboard and **type** the letter **s** (Ctrl + S). This is another way to save your work.

Using Different Views

In Word 7 for Windows 95, you can view your document in several different ways. If you have been following the examples in this book, you have already used Print Preview and Page Layout Views. In this chapter, you will do the following:

✔ View Preview in Page Layout
✔ View Preview in Page Width using the Zoom Control
✔ View Preview at 50%

USING THE VIEW BUTTONS

There are three different buttons in your status bar that provide three different views of your document.

❶ Clicking on this button puts the screen in the Normal View, which is the one you have used throughout this book. It is the view you see when you open Word 7.

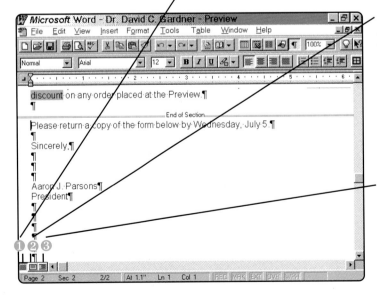

❷ Clicking on this button puts the screen in the Page Layout View that you used in Chapter 8 to create the letterhead design for Preview. You can see graphics, headers, footers, and page numbers in this view.

❸ Clicking on this button puts the screen in the Outline View. In this view, you can collapse a document to see only the main headings or expand it to see the entire document. This view is useful for organizing long documents.

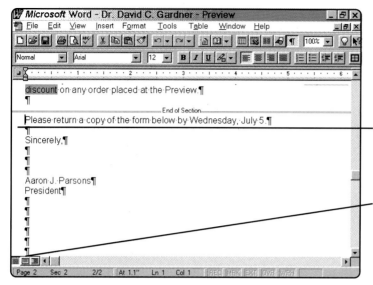

Using Page Layout

1. Click on the ▲ or ▼ on the scroll bar until you can see the top of page 2.

2. Click at the top of page 2 if your cursor is not already there.

3. Click on the **Page Layout button** just above the status bar. Your screen will switch to Page Layout View.

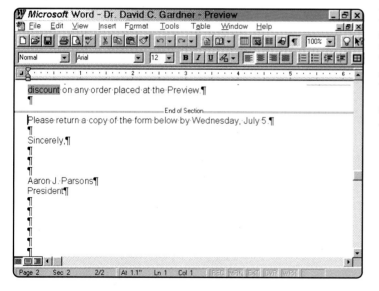

In Page Layout View you can see a document with headers and page numbers as it will look when printed. You can edit the text and change formatting in this view.

USING THE ZOOM COMMAND

The Zoom command controls how large or small a document appears on the screen. You can make a display larger so that it's easier to read or see the details, or reduce the display to view an entire page or two. The Zoom command can be used in all Word 7 views.

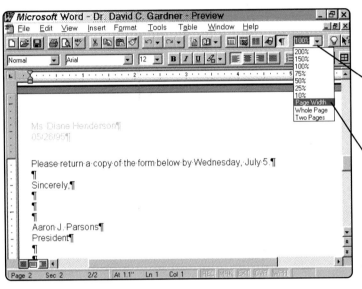

Using Page Width Zoom

1. **Click** on the ▼ next to the Zoom control. The Zoom list will appear.

2. **Click** on **Page Width**. The pull-down list will disappear, and your document will now be shown in page width size.

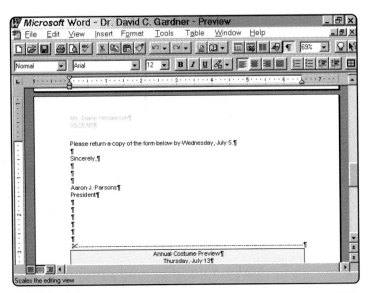

This view enables you to see the entire width of your document. Long sentences will show on the screen and will not scroll out of sight on the right side of your screen. You can work as you always do when in this view.

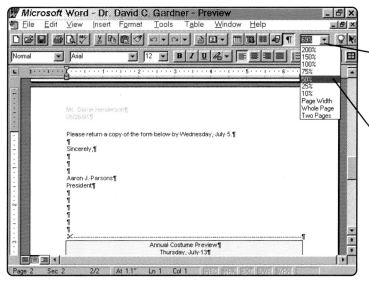

Using 50% Zoom

1. **Click** on the ▼ next to the Zoom control. The Zoom list will appear.

2. **Click** on **50%**. The pull-down list will disappear, and your document will appear in a 50% view.

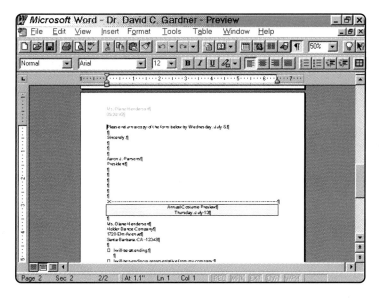

This zoom shows your document in a much reduced size and gives you a bird's-eye view of your document.

Using 100% Zoom and Returning to Normal View

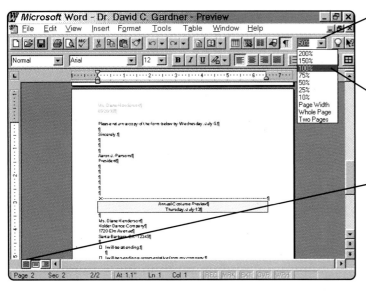

1. **Click** on the ▼ next to the Zoom control. The Zoom list will appear.

2. **Click** on **100%**. The list will disappear, and your document will appear in a 100% view.

3. **Click** on the **Normal View button** above the status bar. The Normal View screen with which you started this chapter will reappear.

Zooming to a Specific Percent

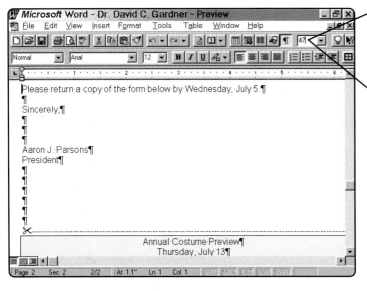

1. **Click** in the **Zoom control box**. The Zoom % number will be highlighted.

2. **Type the number** of the **percent** you want to zoom in or out. In this example, it's 47.

3. **Press Enter**.

Try experimenting with this and in using different views. You will need to return to 100% view for the rest of the examples in this book.

Printing an Envelope and a Label

Word 7 makes it as easy to print an envelope or a label as clicking your mouse. However, to customize an envelope, you must first attach it to a document before you can modify it. In this chapter, you will do the following:

✔ Set up and print an envelope
✔ Permanently customize the return address and print the letter and the envelope at the same time
✔ Print a single label

ENTERING A PERMANENT RETURN ADDRESS

Word 7 automatically places the user information that you entered when you installed Word into the first two lines of the initial envelope return address. The first time you use the envelope program, the two lines will appear unless you modify the user information file. In this section you will open the User Info dialog file and type a permanent address in it.

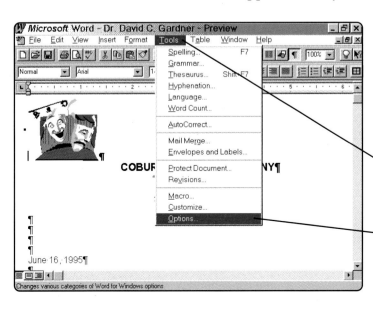

1. **Open Preview** if it isn't already on your screen.

2. **Click** on **Tools** in the menu bar. The Tools menu will appear.

3. **Click** on **Options**. The Options dialog box will appear.

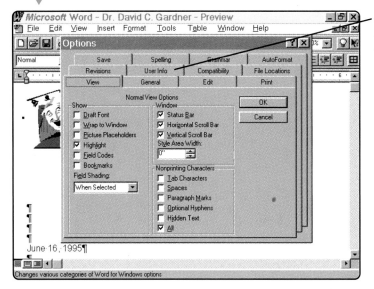

4. Click on the **User Info tab**. The User Info dialog box will come to the front of the Options dialog box.

Notice that the person's name and company used in the installation appears in the mailing address text box.

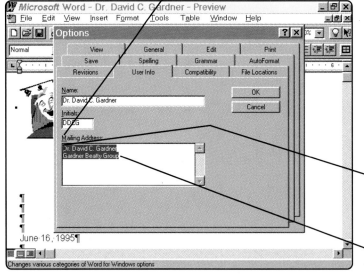

The fact that Word puts this address in a box labeled "mailing address" is confusing. Because this address appears in the upper left corner of the envelope, we will call it the return address.

5. Click in the **Mailing Address box** to set the cursor in the box.

6. Press and hold the **mouse button** and **drag** the cursor to highlight the two lines of text.

7. **Type** your **return address**. In this example, we'll use:

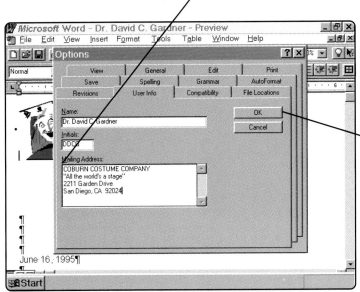

COBURN COSTUME COMPANY
"All the world's a stage"
2211 Garden Drive
San Diego, CA 92024

8. **Click** on **OK**. The **Preview** document will appear.

The return address (mailing address) is now permanently changed.

PRINTING AN ENVELOPE

1. **Click** on **Tools** in the menu bar. The Tools menu will appear.

2. **Click** on **Envelopes and Labels.** The Envelopes and Labels dialog box will appear.

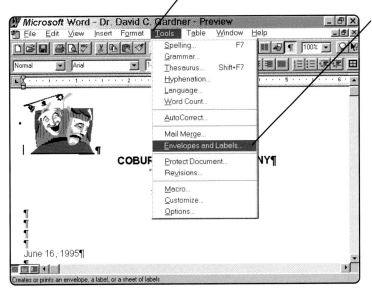

3. **Click** on the **Envelopes tab** to bring it to the front, if necessary.

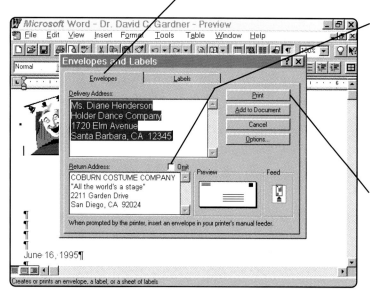

Notice the Omit box above the Return Address. If you are using an envelope with a preprinted return address, click here to place a ✔ in the box. The envelope will print with only the delivery address.

4. **Click** on **Print**.

That's it! That's all you do! The dialog box will close, your envelope will print, and all will be right with the world.

CUSTOMIZING THE ENVELOPE

To permanently change the format of the envelope, you must first attach the envelope to the document.

Notice that on the envelope you just printed, the return address printed in the Arial font. Arial is the standard (default) font that you chose for all documents back in Chapter 1.

Notice also that the size of the font of the return address is rather small. This is because Word has preset the style of the return address to include the size of 10 points.

In the next section, you'll learn how to permanently change the font and font size of the return address.

Attaching the Envelope to a Letter

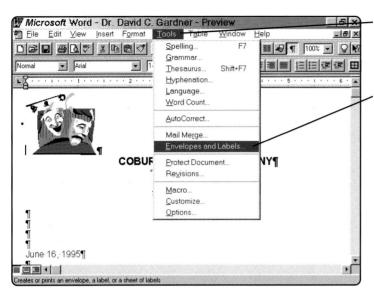

1. **Click** on **Tools** in the menu bar. The Tools menu will appear.

2. **Click** on **Envelopes and Labels**. The Envelopes and Labels dialog box will appear.

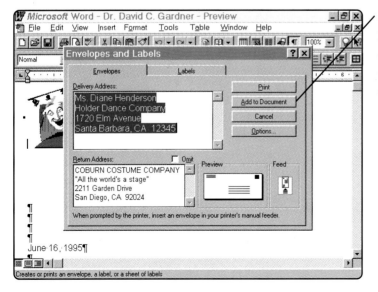

3. **Click** on **Add to Document**. The envelope will appear attached to the top of the first page of the document.

Changing the Envelope Style

1. Click in **front** of **"Coburn"** to set the cursor, if necessary.

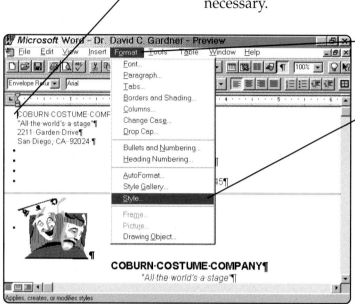

2. Click on **Format** in the menu bar. The Format menu will appear.

3. Click on **Style.** The Style dialog box will appear.

4. Click on **Modify.** The Modify Style dialog box will appear.

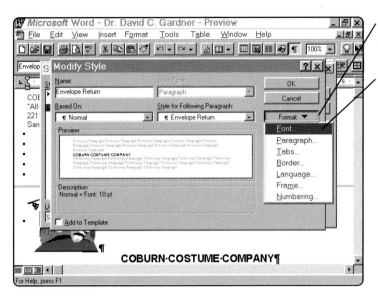

5. Click on **Format.** A pull-down list will appear.

6. Click on **Font.** The Font dialog box will appear.

7. Click repeatedly on the ▼ to scroll to Times New Roman.

8. Click on **Times New Roman** to highlight it.

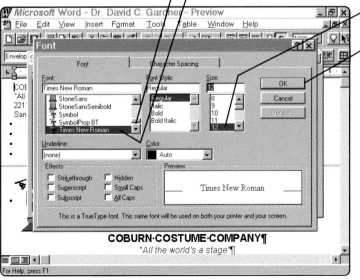

9. Click on **12** to highlight it.

10. Click on **OK.** The Modify Style dialog box will reappear.

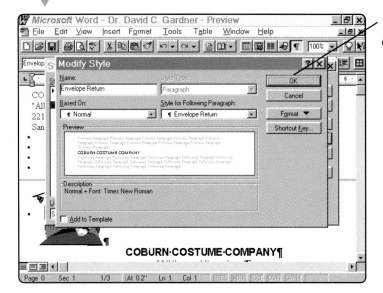

11. **Click** on **OK**. The Style dialog box will appear.

Notice that Envelope Return is highlighted in the Styles box.

12. **Click** on **Apply.** The Style dialog box will close.

The Envelope Return style now includes the Times New Roman font, in 12 points. This is the permanent style for the return address for all future envelopes until you change it.

PRINTING THE LETTER AND THE ATTACHED ENVELOPE

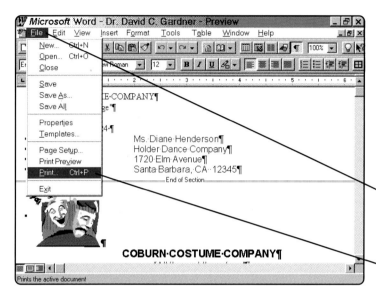

When you print with the Print button, the envelope will automatically be printed first, followed by the letter. If you want to print only the letter or only the envelope, go to the sections that follow this one.

1. **Click** on **File** in the menu bar. The File menu will appear.

2. **Click** on **Print.** The Print dialog box will appear.

3. **Click** on **All** to place a dot in the circle if the dot is not already there.

4. **Click** on **OK.** The envelope and all pages of the document will print.

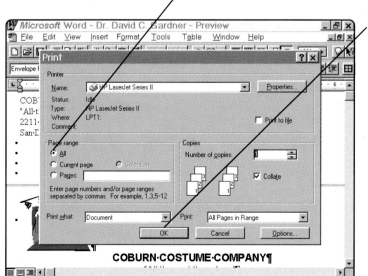

PRINTING THE ATTACHED ENVELOPE WITHOUT THE LETTER

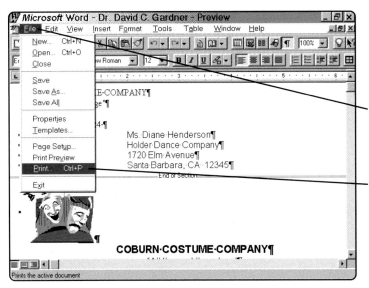

When you attach an envelope to a Word document, the envelope becomes page "0" of the document

1. **Click** on **File** in the menu bar. The File menu will appear.

2. **Click** on **Print.** The Print dialog box will appear.

3. **Click** on **Pages** to put a dot in the circle. The cursor will flash in the Pages text box.

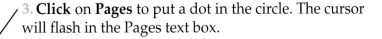

4. **Type** a **0** (zero) in the Pages box.

5. **Click** on **OK.** The envelope will print.

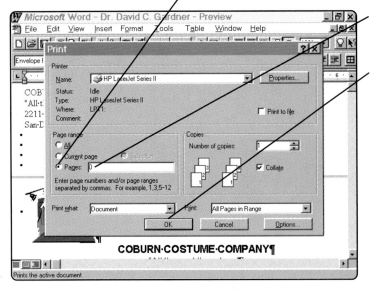

PRINTING THE LETTER WITHOUT THE ATTACHED ENVELOPE

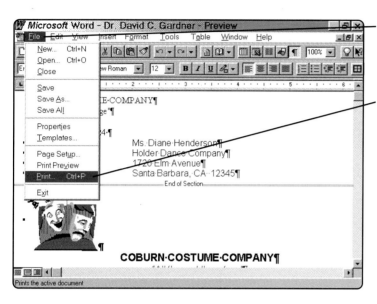

1. **Click** on **File** in the menu bar. The File menu will appear.

2. **Click** on **Print.** The Print dialog box will appear.

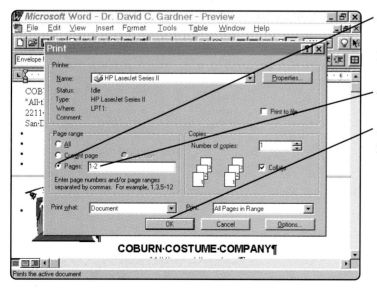

3. **Click** on **Pages** to place a dot in the circle if the dot is not already there.

4. **Type 1-2** in the Pages box.

5. **Click** on **OK.** The pages in the document will print.

CLOSING THE LETTER WITHOUT THE ATTACHED ENVELOPE

If you save the changes you've made to your document up to this point, your document will always appear with the envelope at the top of the letter. In this example, we will close the document without saving the attached envelope.

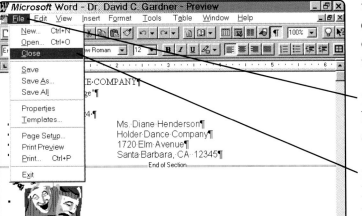

1. **Click** on **File** in the menu bar. The File menu will appear.

2. **Click** on **Close**. A Microsoft Word dialog box will appear.

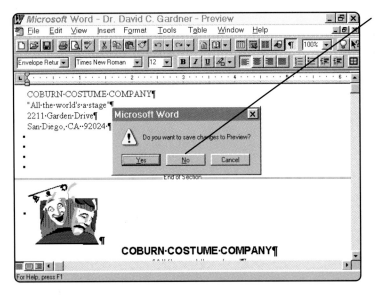

3. **Click** on **No.** The letter will close, and the envelope will not be attached when you reopen the letter.

USING LABELS

The Labels dialog box will automatically show the address with the same font, size, and style as the address in your letter. To change the font, size, or style of the address on your label, you must change it on the letter first. In this example, you'll use the same styles as are in the letter.

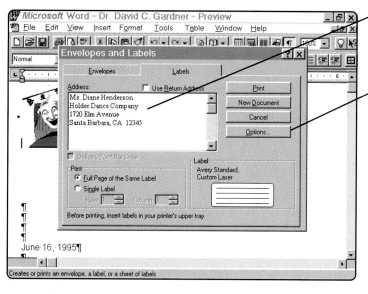

1. **Open Preview**, if it's not already on your screen.

2. **Click** on **Tools** in the menu bar. The Tools menu will appear.

3. **Click** on **Envelopes and Labels.** The Envelopes and Labels dialog box will appear.

Notice that the delivery address shows in the text box.

4. **Click** on **Options**. The Label Options dialog box will appear.

Choosing the Label Size

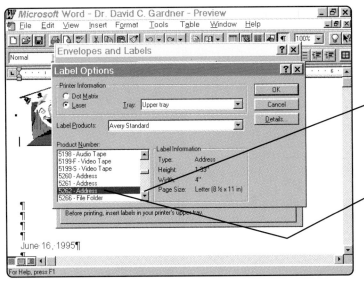

If you're using a different brand of labels than the standard Avery, choose an Avery label of the same size.

1. **Click repeatedly** on the ▼ on the scroll bar to scroll through the list of Product Numbers.

2. **Click** on **5262 - Address** to highlight it.

3. **Click** on **OK**. The dialog box will close.

Printing a Single Label

1. **Click** on **Single Label** to put a dot in the circle.

2. **Click twice** on the ▲ to the right of the Row text box. The row number will change to 3.

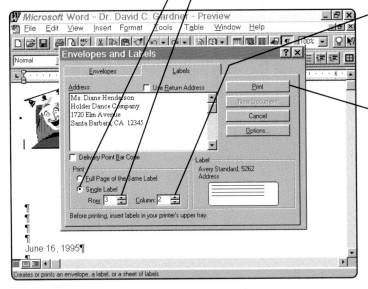

3. **Click** on the ▲ to the right of the Column text box. The column number will change to 2.

4. **Click** on **Print**. The dialog box will close, and the label will print three labels down from the top, on the right side of the label sheet.

5. **Repeat steps 1 through 3** in the "Closing the Letter Without the Attached Envelope" section to close Preview.

WORD FOR WINDOWS 95

Part III: Mailing Lists, Form Letters, Labels, and Envelopes

Introducing Mail Merge

In some previous versions of Word, Mail Merge was called Print Merge. Whatever it's called, it lets you send a personalized version of the same letter to a number of people on a list. You first create the letter, called a *main document*. Then, you create a mailing list, called a *data source*. Next, you tell Word where to substitute information from the mailing list for information in the letter. This process is called *inserting field codes*. Finally, Word will combine the letter and the mailing list, and print the personalized letters. In this chapter, you'll explore all the steps needed to create a Mail Merged document.

STEP #1: CREATING A LETTER

The first step in setting up a mailing is to create the letter that will be personalized and sent to each person on your list. This letter is called the *main document*. You created a letter in chapters 1 through 10 that will be used to do a mailing.

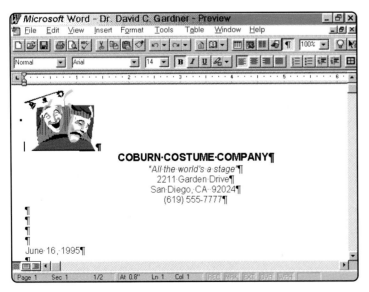

STEP #2:
CREATING A LIST OF NAMES

The second step in Mail Merge is to create a list of names and addresses, called a *data file*. The information in the list is put into categories, or *fields*, such as Last Name, First Name, Company, etc. You will create a data file in Chapter 14, "Creating a Mailing List."

STEP #3: CODING THE LETTER

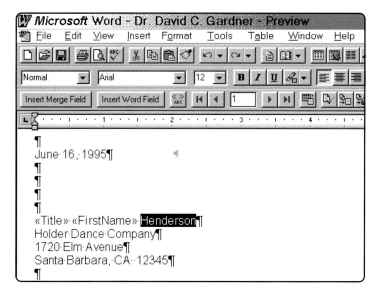

The next step in the process is to put special codes into the letter that tell Word where to insert information (*fields*) from the mailing list into the letter. In Chapter 15, you'll learn how to insert a special code for "first name," for example, into a spot where the recipient's first name will appear in the letter. This sounds complicated, but we'll give you easy step-by-step directions.

STEP #4:
MAIL MERGING THE LETTERS

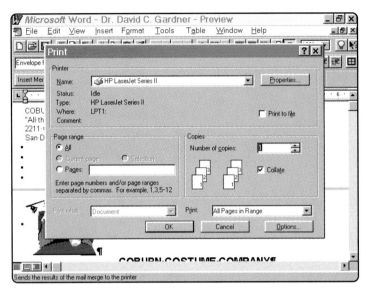

In this step, Word actually combines the original coded letter, or *main document* and the mailing list, or the *data source*.

In the previous step, you told Word which parts of the letter to replace with information from the mailing list. In this step, you simply click on the Merge to Printer button on the mail merge toolbar. Word automatically prints a personalized letter for each person on the mailing list.

STEP #5:
CODING ENVELOPES AND LABELS

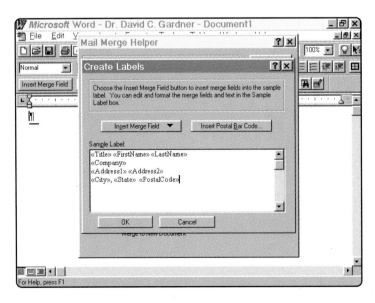

You can Mail Merge envelopes and labels for the names in your list. In Chapter 15, you'll learn to print the envelopes along with the letters. In Chapter 16, you'll learn how to print labels or envelopes separately for a mailing list.

Creating a Mailing List

With Word's mail merge feature, you can send the same letter (a form letter, for example) to different people and have the individual's name, address, salutation, and other information personalized on each letter without having to retype each one. After you have written the letter, begin the mail merge process by creating a mailing list. In this chapter, you will do the following:

✔ Create a mailing list table of names and addresses, called a Data Source

GETTING READY TO CREATE A MAILING LIST

In this example, you'll go through a series of dialog boxes in order to tell Word that you want to create a mailing list.

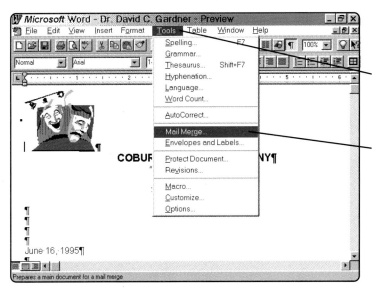

1. **Open** the **Preview** file if it's not already open.

2. **Click** on **Tools** in the menu bar. The Tools menu will appear.

3. **Click** on **Mail Merge**. The Mail Merge Helper dialog box will appear.

4. **Click** on **Create**. The Create menu will appear.

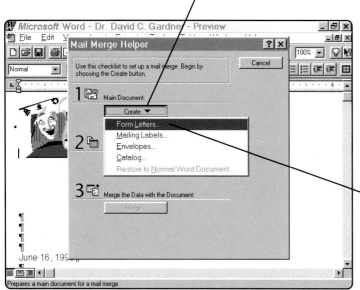

Note: For some reason, Word insists that you tell it what kind of document you're going to use the list with. You must attach the data source to a document *before* you create the data source.

5. **Click** on **Form Letters**. A Microsoft Word dialog box will appear.

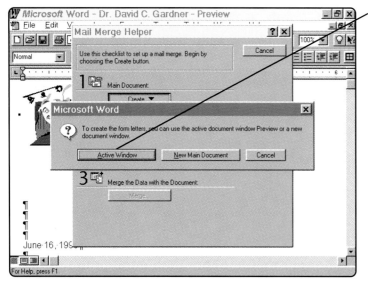

6. **Click** on **Active Window**. The Mail Merge Helper dialog box will appear.

Note: You are selecting this option because you want to use the Preview document that is on your screen. In other words, you want to use the *Active Window*.

7. **Click** on **Get Data**. The Get Data menu will appear.

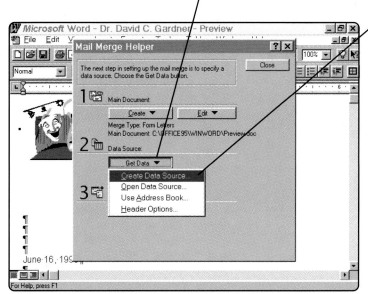

8. **Click** on **Create Data Source**. The Create Data Source dialog box will appear.

CREATING A DATA SOURCE

In Word, a mailing list is put in the form of a table. Each column in the table contains a different category, or *field*, of information, such as last name, street, zip code, etc. The first row in the table is called the *header row*. The header row contains the names of the fields.

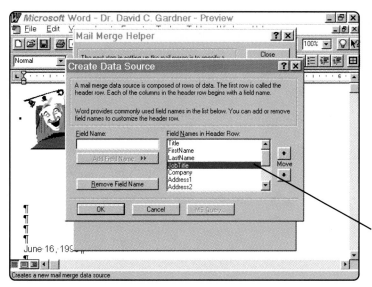

Word provides you with a built-in list of field names. You can accept, rename, delete from, or add to, the list of field names to create a customized mailing list.

Removing Field Names

1. **Click** on **Job Title** to highlight it.

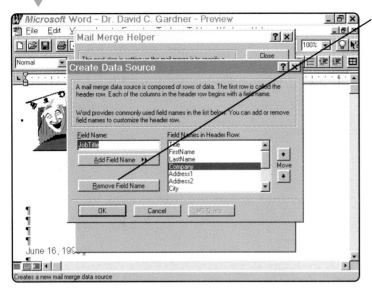

2. Click on **Remove Field Name.** Job Title will move to the Field Name text box.

3. Press the **Delete key** on your keyboard. Job Title will disappear. The Field Name text box will be blank with the cursor flashing in it.

4. Click repeatedly on the ▼ on the scroll bar to scroll to the bottom of the list.

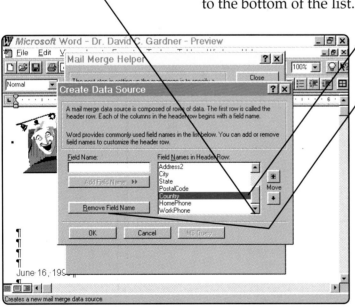

5. Click on **Country** to highlight it.

6. Click on **Remove Field Name.** Country will move to the Field Name text box.

7. Press the **Delete key** on your keyboard. Country will disappear. The Field Name text box will be blank with the cursor flashing in it.

Adding a Field Name

If you're following along with this book, your cursor is already in the Field Name text box.

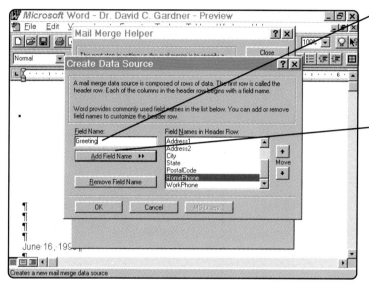

1. **Click** in the **Field Name** text box to place the cursor, if necessary.

2. **Type Greeting**.

3. **Click** on **Add Field Name**. The new header field name, Greeting, will be added to the bottom of the Field Name list box.

Notice that Greeting is now at the bottom of the Field Name list.

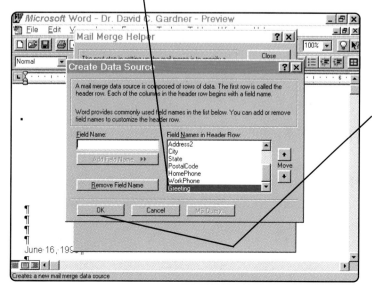

SAVING THE DATA SOURCE FILE

1. **Click** on **OK**. The Save As dialog box will appear.

2. **Type My List** (Word will automatically add the .doc extension).

3. **Click** on **Save**. After a pause, a Microsoft Word dialog box will appear.

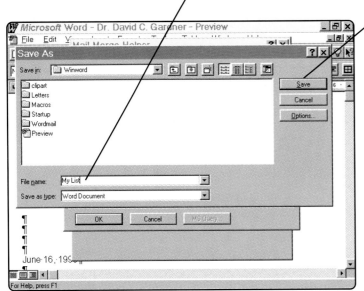

ENTERING NAMES AND ADDRESSES IN THE DATA SOURCE TABLE

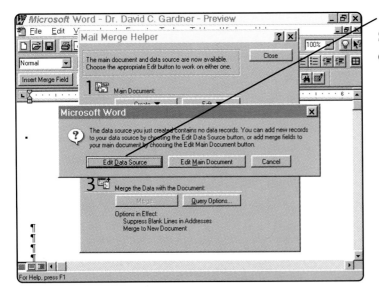

1. **Click** on **Edit Data Source**. The Data Form dialog box will appear.

2. **Type Ms.** and **press** the **Enter key**. The cursor will move to the FirstName text box.

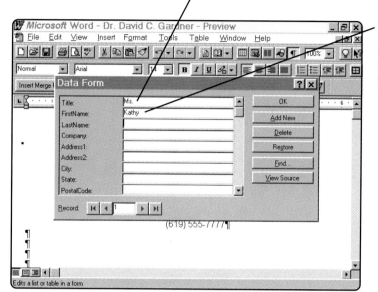

3. **Type Kathy** and **press** the **Enter key**. The cursor will move to the LastName text box.

4. **Repeat step 2** to type the following information in the data entry text boxes:

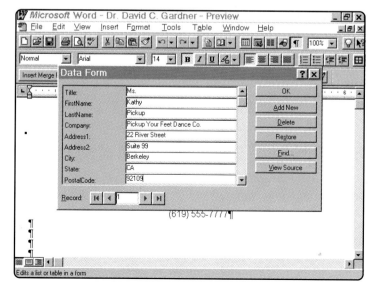

Pickup

Pickup Your Feet Dance Co.

22 River Street

Suite 99

Berkeley

CA

92109

5. **Click** on the ▼ to scroll to the bottom of the list of field names.

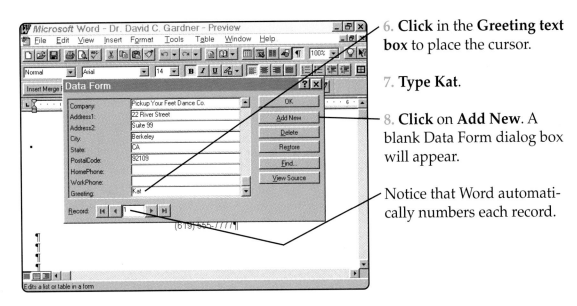

6. **Click** in the **Greeting text box** to place the cursor.

7. **Type Kat**.

8. **Click** on **Add New**. A blank Data Form dialog box will appear.

Notice that Word automatically numbers each record.

9. **Repeat steps 2 and 3** to type the following information:

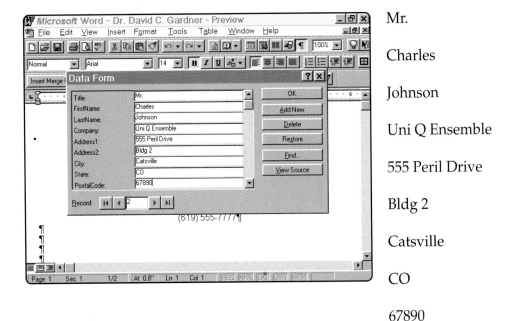

Mr.

Charles

Johnson

Uni Q Ensemble

555 Peril Drive

Bldg 2

Catsville

CO

67890

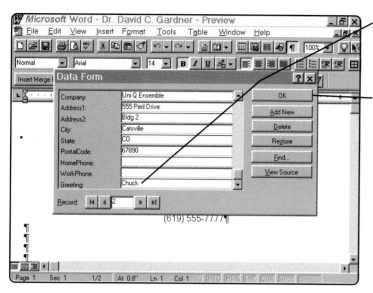

10. **Repeat steps 5 through 7** to type Chuck in the Greeting text box.

11. **Click** on **OK**. The Data Form dialog box will close.

VIEWING THE DATA SOURCE

Notice that the mail merge toolbar has automatically appeared.

You have just set up a Data Source table for your mailing list, entered the names and addresses of two people, and what do you see? The Preview document screen with a new toolbar! Just hang in there. These next steps will show you exactly what you have accomplished.

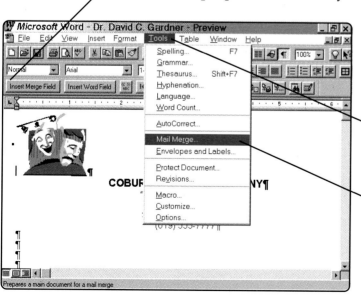

1. **Click** on **Tools** in the menu bar. The Tools menu will appear.

2. **Click** on **Mail Merge**. The Mail Merge Helper dialog box will appear.

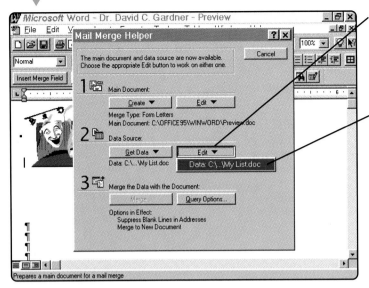

3. Click on the **Edit button** to the right of Get Data. A pull-down list of data source files will appear.

4. Click on **Data: C:\...\My List.doc**. The Data Form dialog box will appear.

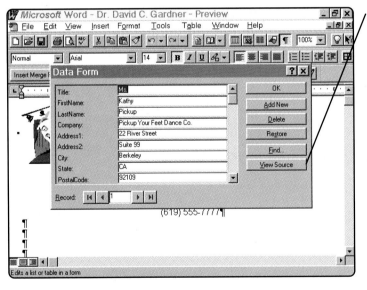

5. Click on **View Source**. Voilà! The data source table you created, along with the addresses you entered, will appear!

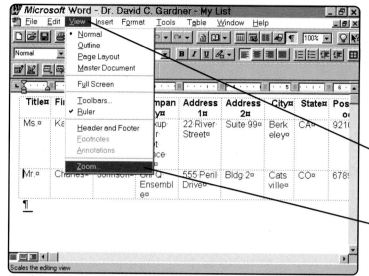

Improving the View

You can't see the entire table, but you can fix the view with just a few mouse clicks.

1. **Click** on **View** in the menu bar. The View menu will appear.

2. **Click** on **Zoom**. The Zoom dialog box will appear.

3. **Click** on **Page Width** to place a dot in the circle.

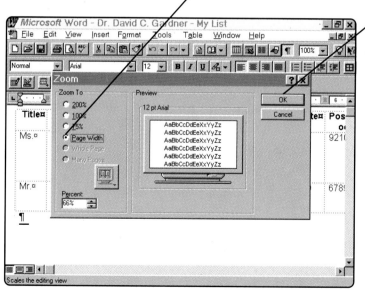

4. **Click** on **OK**. The dialog box will close.

Note: Don't worry that the spacing in some of the columns looks weird. The information will print correctly in the letters.

SAVING AND CLOSING
THE MAILING LIST

1. **Click** on **File** in the menu bar. The File menu will appear.

2. **Click** on **Close**. A Microsoft Word dialog box will appear.

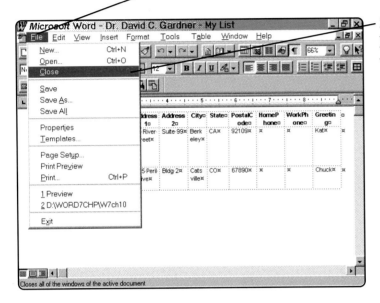

3. **Click** on **Yes**. The Preview document window will appear.

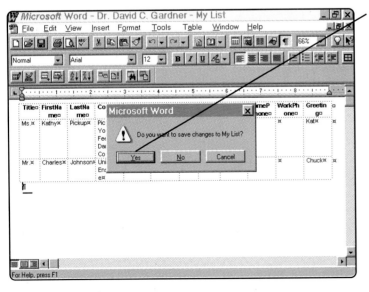

4. **Click** on **File** in the menu bar. The File menu will appear.

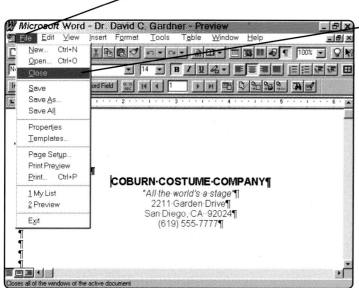

5. **Click** on **Close**. A Microsoft Word dialog box will appear.

Note: In Word you cannot create a data source table or use the mail merge toolbar unless the data source table is attached to a document. In this example, Preview was used solely to create the data source table, My List.doc. Because no changes were made to Preview, you don't need to save it now that the My List.doc has been created and saved.

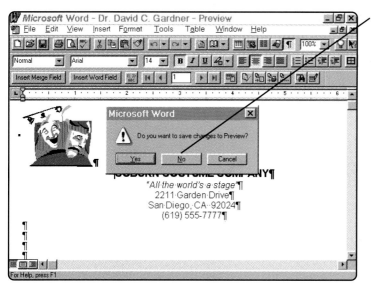

6. **Click** on **No**. Preview will close, and an empty Word screen will appear.

If not saving makes you feel anxious, click on Yes.

Setting Up and Mail Merging Form Letters and Envelopes

In Chapter 14 you completed your mailing list by adding new fields and data. You are now ready to code the letter to match the mailing list so that it will print personalized letters and envelopes. In this chapter, you will do the following:

✔ Code a form letter
✔ Merge print the form letters and envelopes

ATTACHING A MAILING LIST FILE TO A LETTER

1. **Open Preview** if it is not already on your screen.

2. **Click** on **Tools**. The Tools menu will appear.

3. **Click** on **Mail Merge**. The Mail Merge Helper dialog box will appear.

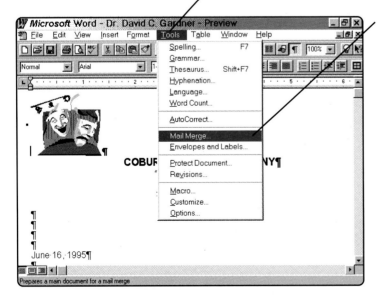

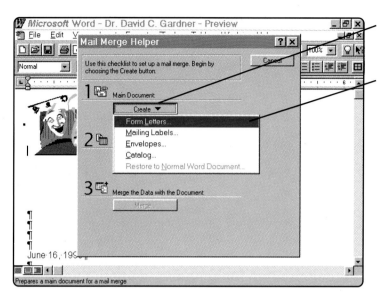

4. Click on **Create.** A pull-down list will appear.

5. Click on **Form Letters**. The Microsoft Word dialog box will appear.

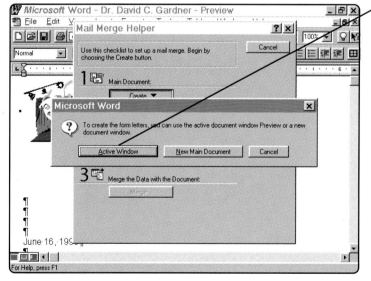

6. Click on **Active Window**. The Mail Merge Helper dialog box will appear.

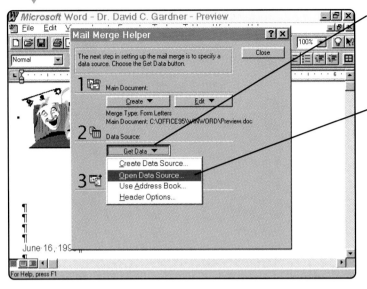

7. **Click** on **Get Data** in the Data Source text box. A pull-down menu will appear.

8. **Click** on **Open Data Source.** The Open Data Source dialog box will appear.

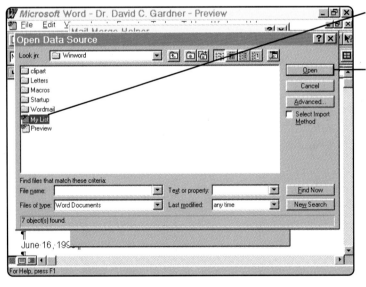

9. **Click** on **My List** to highlight it.

10. **Click** on **Open**. A Microsoft Word dialog box will appear.

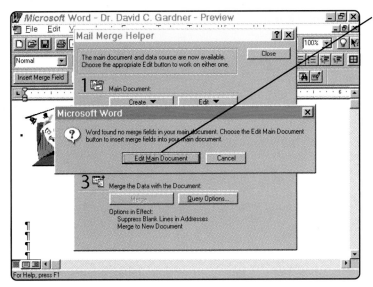

11. **Click** on **Edit Main Document**. The Preview document will appear on your screen.

INSERTING MERGE FIELDS INTO A FORM LETTER

1. **Click repeatedly** on the ▼ on the scroll bar to see the address as you see in this example.

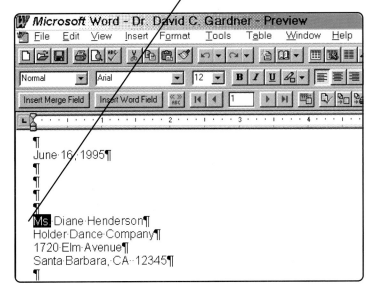

2. **Click** to place the cursor to the **left of "Ms."**

3. **Press and hold** the **mouse button** as you **drag** to the right to highlight **"Ms."** Be careful to high-light the period (.) but *not* the space after it.

4. **Release** the **mouse button**.

5. **Click** on **Insert Merge Field.** A list of field names will appear.

6. **Click** on **Title**. The "Ms." prefix will be replaced with the merge field <<Title>>. This means that when you print the form letter, the title (Dr., Mrs., Mr., etc.) will be inserted in the letter for each person on the list.

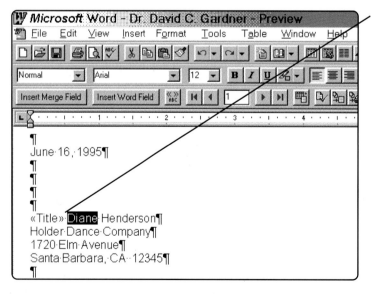

7. **Click** to place the cursor to the **left** of **"Diane"**

8. **Press and hold** the **mouse button** as you **drag** to the right to highlight **"Diane."** Then **release** the **mouse button.**

You could, of course, place the cursor on top of the word, then click twice to highlight the word. However, this action normally highlights both the word *and* the space after it. We recommend the "drag" method of highlighting so that you don't accidently delete spaces between words.

9. **Click** on **Insert Merge Field.** A list of field names will appear.

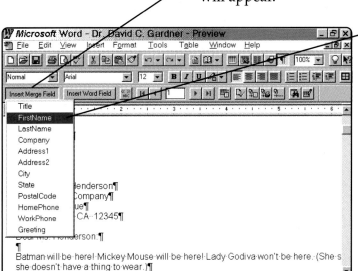

10. **Click** on **FirstName.** "Diane" will be replaced with the merge field <<FirstName>>. This means that when you print the form letter, the first name of each person in your mailing list will be inserted in the letter printed for that person.

Make sure that there is one space between <<Title>> and <<FirstName>>.

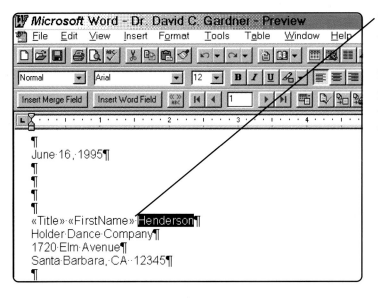

11. **Click** to place the cursor to the **left of "Henderson."**

12. **Press and hold** the **mouse button** as you **drag** to the right to highlight **"Henderson."**

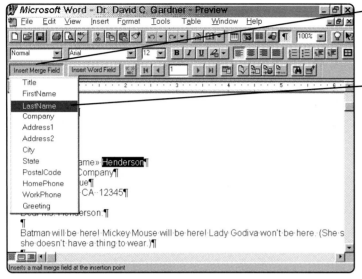

13. Click on **Insert Merge Field.** A list of field names will appear.

14. Click on **LastName.** "Henderson" will be replaced with the merge field <<LastName>>. This means that when you print the form letter, the last name of each person in your mailing list will be inserted in the letter printed for that person.

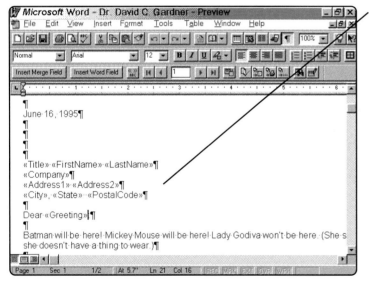

15. Repeat steps 2 through 6 to insert the other merge field codes into the remaining address and salutation sections of the form letter. Add the <<Address2>> merge field to the street address line to allow for suite numbers in your mailing list. Make certain you don't highlight the comma after "Santa Barbara" or the colon after "Henderson." Be sure to highlight both "Ms." and "Henderson" and replace it with the merge field "Greeting."

If you goof and put a merge field in the wrong place, click on the Undo button to remove the incorrect merge field and repeat steps 2 through 6 to insert the correct merge field. Be careful not to add or delete spaces.

Inserting Personalized Information into the Body of the Letter

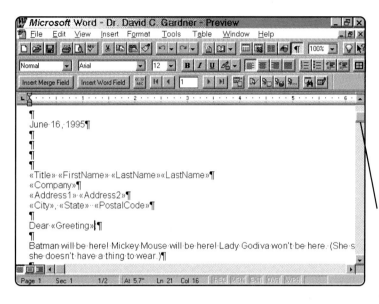

Just as you've personalized the letter by adding a name, address, and greeting to the first page of the letter, you can also insert personal touches in the body of the letter using the same kinds of fields used on page 1 of the letter.

1. Press and hold on the **button** on the scroll bar as you drag the button approximately halfway down the scroll bar to bring the bottom of page 1 into view.

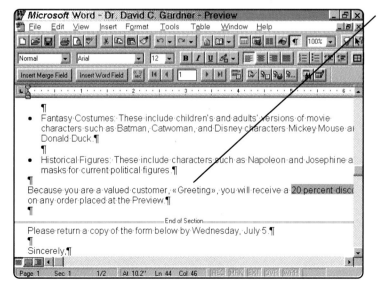

2. Repeat steps 2 through 6 in the previous section "Inserting Merge Fields into a Form Letter" to insert the <<Greeting>> merge field.

Inserting Personalized Information into the Header

1. **Click anywhere** on page 2 to access the page 2 header you inserted in Chapter 10.

2. **Click** on **View** in the menu bar. The View menu will appear.

3. **Click** on **Header and Footer**. The header and footer toolbar will appear.

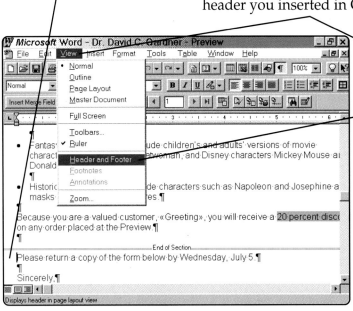

4. **Repeat steps 1 through 6** in the section entitled "Inserting Merge Fields into a Form Letter" to insert the <<Title>> merge field.

5. **Repeat steps 7 through 14** in the same section to insert the <<First Name>> and <<Last Name>> merge fields.

Note: Make sure there is a space after <<Title>> and after <<FirstName>>.

6. **Click** on **Close**. The header and footer toolbar will close, and Preview will reappear on your screen at page 2.

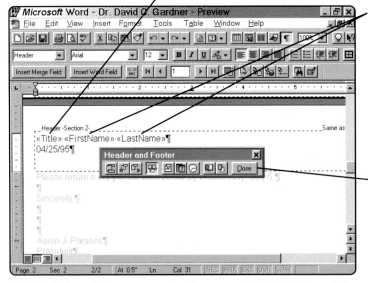

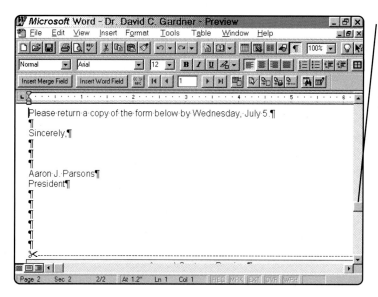

7. **Press and hold** on the **scroll button** as you **drag** the button down the scroll bar to bring the address on page 2 into view.

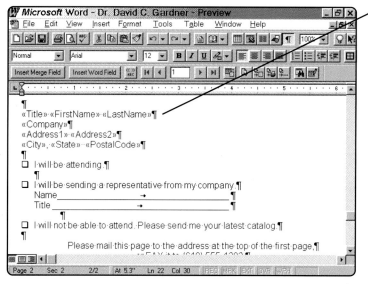

8. **Repeat steps 2 through 15** in the section entitled "Inserting Merge Fields into a Form Letter" once again to insert the merge field codes into the reply form on page 2.

Note: If you're feeling adventurous, try this:

A. **Copy** the four lines of **merge fields** you inserted.

B. **Highlight** the four lines of **address** on page 2.

C. While the four lines on page 2 are highlighted, **click** on the **Paste button** on the toolbar. The copied merge fields will replace the highlighted text.

See the section entitled "Copying and Pasting Text" in Chapter 6 if you need help.

ATTACHING THE ENVELOPE TO THE FORM LETTER

In this section, you will attach the envelope to the form letter. This will first print the envelope and then the letter, in sequence, for each person on the list.

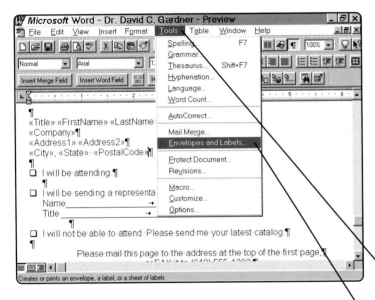

Note: Attaching the envelope works beautifully if you have an automatic envelope feeder. If you don't have an envelope feeder, you must stand by your printer and manually feed in the envelopes.

To learn how to print Mail Merged envelopes without letters, see Chapter 16.

1. Click on **Tools** in the menu bar. The Tools menu will appear.

2. Click on **Envelopes and Labels**. The Envelopes and Labels dialog box will appear.

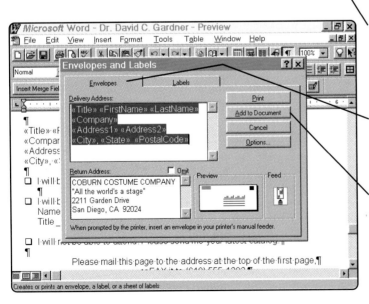

3. Click on the **Envelopes tab** to bring it to the front, if necessary.

4. Click on **Add to Document**. The dialog box will close, and the envelope will appear at the top of the document, complete with merge fields in place.

PRINTING THE FORM LETTERS AND ENVELOPES

With this method of combining the letter and envelope, if you don't have an automatic feeder, you'll need to manually feed the envelopes between the letters.

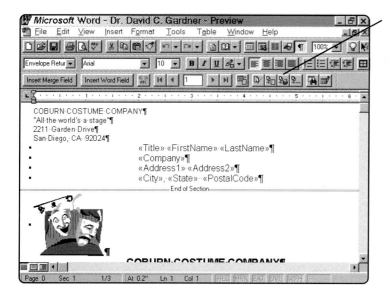

1. Click on the **Merge to Printer button.** The Print dialog box will appear.

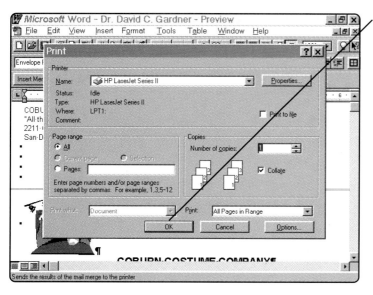

2. Click on **OK.** A Printing message dialog box will appear.

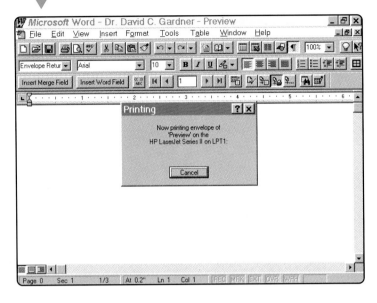

The Printing message box will stay on the screen until the envelopes and both pages of the document have been sent to the printer. Your printer will now print two, two-page form letters and their envelopes using the personalized information that you entered into the My List mailing list file.

Isn't this great?

SAVING YOUR FORM LETTER

Make sure you save the coded letter. After all the work you've done, it would be a shame to lose it.

1. **Click** on **File** in the menu bar. The File Menu will appear.

2. **Click** on **Save As**. The Save As dialog box will appear.

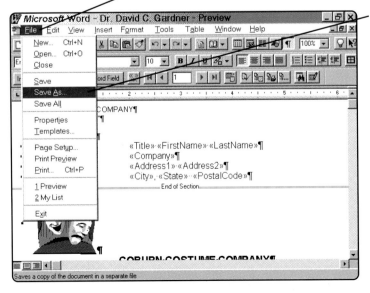

3. **Type My Form** in the File name box.

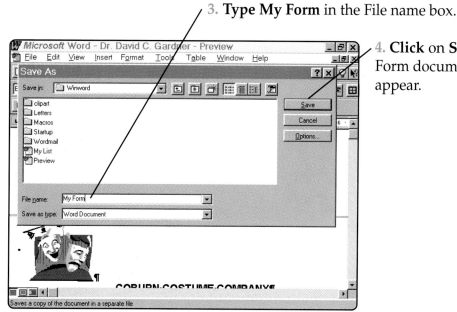

4. **Click** on **Save**. The My Form document will appear.

Closing the Form Letter

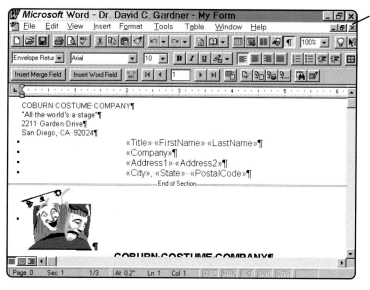

1. **Click** on the **Close Document button** on the far right of the menu bar. My Form will close, and you will be returned to an empty Word screen.

Mail Merging Labels and Envelopes for a Mailing List

You can print labels and envelopes from any mailing list totally separate from any form letter connected to the mailing list. You do this by creating and saving a merge printing label or envelope document set up to print from a specific mailing list. We recommend printing envelopes from a long mailing list only if you have an envelope feeder for your printer or tractor feed envelopes. In this chapter, you will do the following:

✔ Create a label document file for printing labels from a mailing list
✔ Print labels from a mailing list
✔ Print a specific envelope from a mailing list

CREATING A LABEL DOCUMENT FILE FOR A MAILING LIST

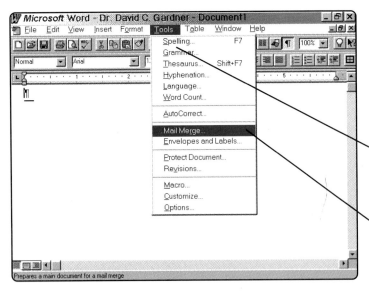

Click on the New button on the toolbar to open a new document if one is not already on your screen. It's the first button on the toolbar.

1. **Click** on **Tools** in the menu bar. The Tools menu will appear.

2. **Click** on **Mail Merge**. The Mail Merge Helper dialog box will appear.

3. **Click** on **Create**. A pull-down list will appear.

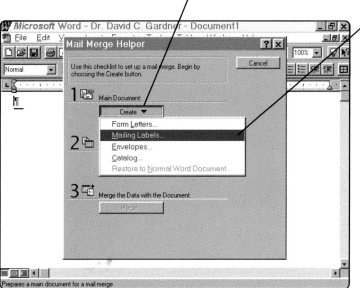

4. **Click** on **Mailing Labels**. A Microsoft Word dialog box will appear.

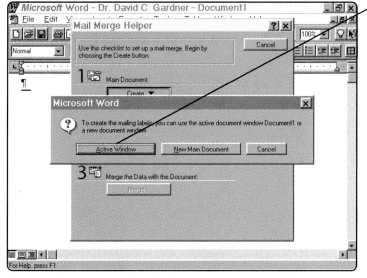

5. **Click** on **Active Window**. The Mail Merge Helper dialog box will appear.

6. **Click** on **Get Data**. A pull-down list will appear.

7. **Click** on **Open Data Source**. The Open Data Source dialog box will appear.

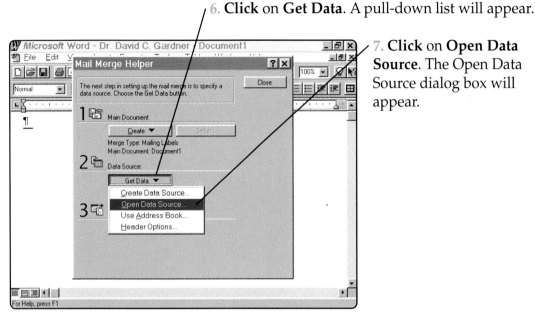

8. **Click** on **My List** to highlight it.

9. **Click** on **Open**. A Microsoft Word dialog box will appear.

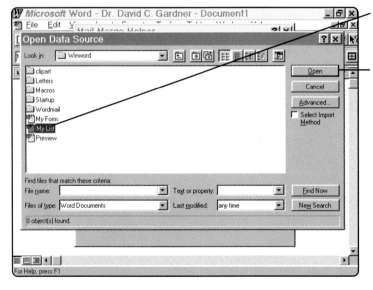

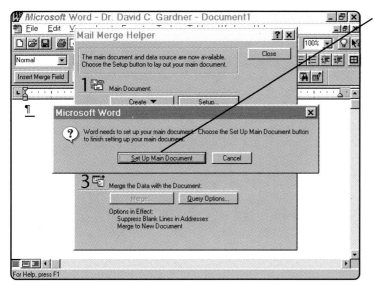

10. Click on **Set Up Main Document**. The Label Options dialog box will appear.

CHOOSING A LABEL SIZE

Notice the Printer Information area. Laser is the standard (default) type of printer. In this example, we'll leave Laser selected.

1. Click on the ▼ to the right of Label Products. The Label Products menu will appear.

Notice that Avery Standard appears highlighted. Word is set up to print on most sizes of Avery brand labels. If you're printing on another brand of labels, you can click on Other to bring up another list in the Product Number list. Or, you can choose an Avery label of the same size.

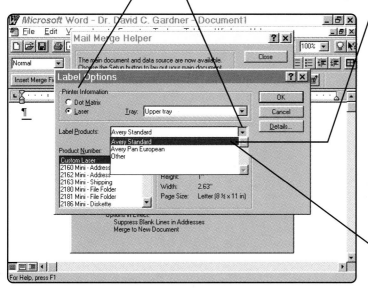

2. Click on **Avery Standard**. Avery Standard will reappear in the Label Products text box.

3. **Click repeatedly** on the ▼ on the scroll bar to scroll through the Product Number list.

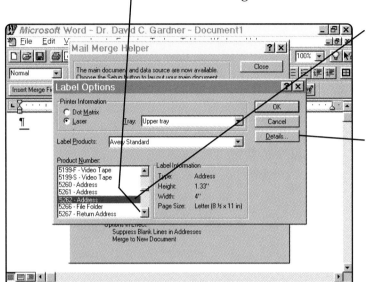

4. **Click** on **5262-Address** to highlight it. The Label Information to the right will change to show you the dimensions of the label.

5. **Click** on **Details**. The Address 5262 Information dialog box will appear.

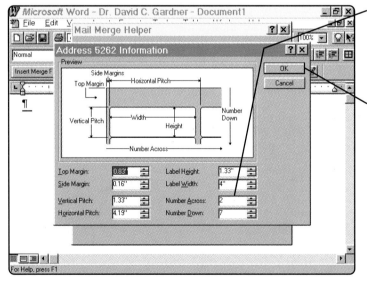

Notice that this dialog box lists additional information about the 5262-Address labels.

6. **Click** on **OK**. The dialog box will close, and the Label Options dialog box will appear.

7. **Click** on **OK** on the **Label Options** dialog box. The dialog box will close, and the Create Labels dialog box will appear.

INSERTING MERGE FIELD NAMES INTO THE LABEL

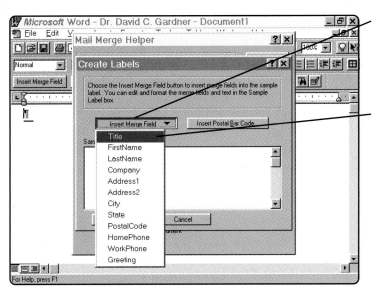

1. **Click** on **Insert Merge Field**. A pull-down list of merge field names will appear.

2. **Click** on **Title**. <<Title>> will appear in the Sample Label text box.

3. **Press** the **Spacebar.**

4. **Repeat steps 1 through 3** to place the **<<FirstName>>** and **<<LastName>>** field in the Sample Label text box.

5. **Press** the **Enter key.** The cursor will move to the next line of the address.

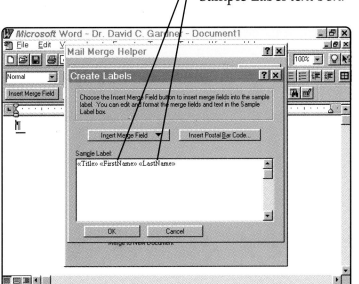

6. **Repeat steps 1 through 3** in this section to insert the remaining merge fields in the Sample Label text box.

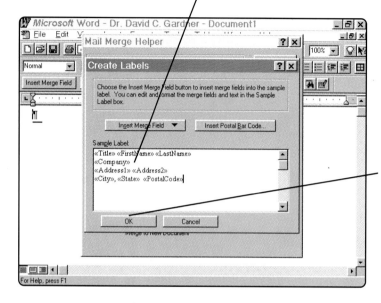

Press the Enter key at the end of each line. Insert a comma followed by a space after the <<City>> field. Put two spaces between the <<State>> and <<PostalCode>> fields.

7. **Click** on **OK**. The Mail Merge Helper dialog box will appear.

MERGE PRINTING LABELS WITH THE ENTIRE MAILING LIST

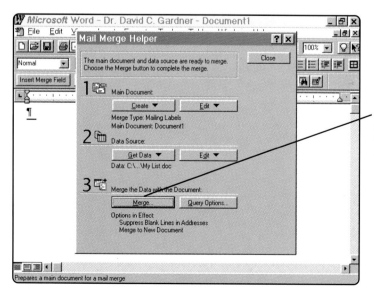

Load the blank labels into your printer tray or put tractor feed labels in your dot-matrix printer.

1. **Click** on **Merge**. The Merge dialog box will appear.

2. **Click** on the ▼ to the right of the Merge To list box. A pull-down list will appear.

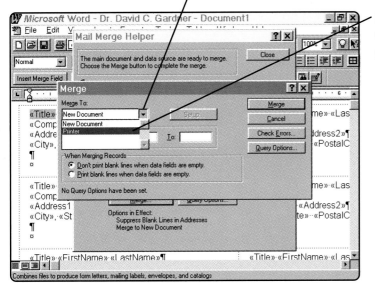

3. **Click** on **Printer**. Printer will appear in the Merge To text box.

4. **Click** on **Merge**. The Print dialog box will appear.

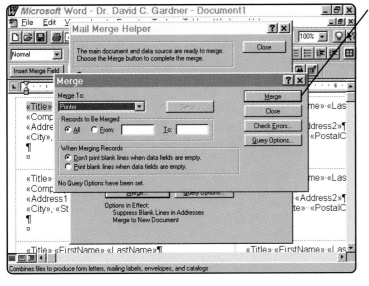

5. **Click** on **All** to place a dot in the circle if one is not already there.

6. **Click** on **OK**. A Printing message box will appear.

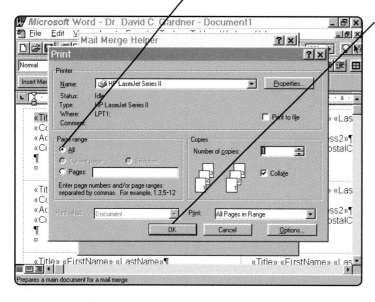

The Printing message box will appear on the screen.

When the labels have printed, the Printing message box and the Mail Merge Helper dialog box will close.

The *unsaved* merge label screen will appear.

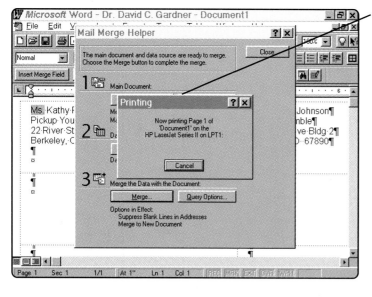

SAVING THE LABEL DOCUMENT FILE

It's important to save this label setup if you want to use it again.

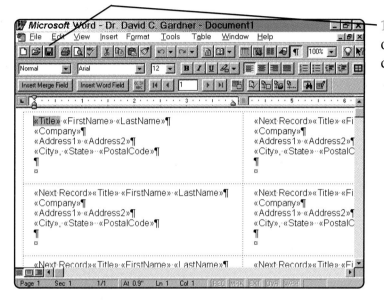

1. Click on the **Save button** on the toolbar. The Save As dialog box will appear.

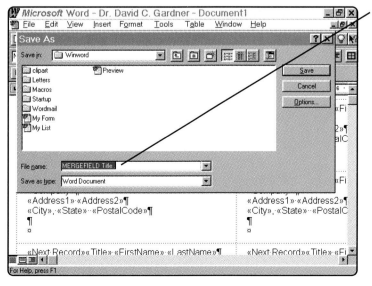

Word's name for this type of file, MERGEFIELD Title, will be highlighted in the File name text box.

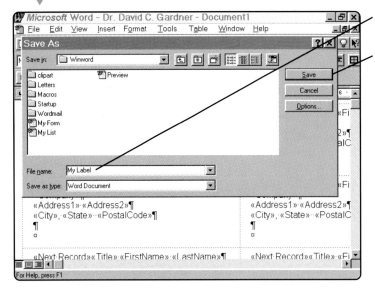

2. **Type My Label.**

3. **Click** on **Save**. The My Label window will appear.

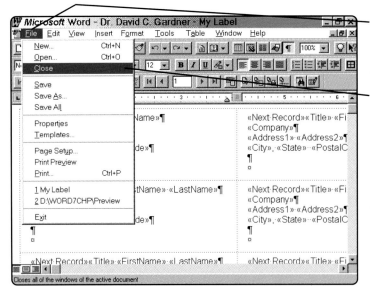

4. **Click** on **File** in the menu bar. The File menu will appear.

5. **Click** on **Close**. My Label will close and an empty Word screen will appear.

CREATING AN ENVELOPE DOCUMENT FILE FOR A MAILING LIST

You use the same procedure to mail merge envelopes as you do for labels. In this example, we'll show you only the envelope screens that are different from the label screens.

1. **Open** a **new document.**

2. **Repeat steps 1 and 2** at the beginning of this chapter to bring the Mail Merge Helper dialog box into view.

3. **Click** on **Create.**

4. **Click** on **Envelopes.** A dialog box will appear.

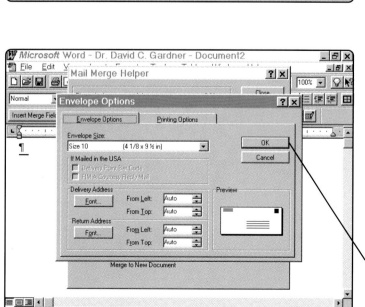

5. **Repeat steps 5 through 10** in the same section to bring the Envelope Options dialog box into view, this time choosing Envelopes.

Notice that you can make style changes to your envelope with this dialog box.

6. **Click** on **OK.** The Envelope Address dialog box will appear.

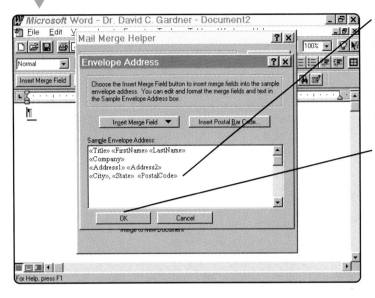

7. **Repeat steps 1 through 7** in the section entitled "Inserting Merge Field Names Into the Label" to insert the merge field names into the envelope.

8. **Click** on **OK**. The Mail Merge Helper dialog box will appear.

Insert the envelope tray into your laser printer or put tractor feed envelopes in your dot-matrix printer.

9. **Repeat steps 1 through 6** in the section entitled "Merge Printing Labels with the Entire Mailing List." The Printing message box will appear on the screen.

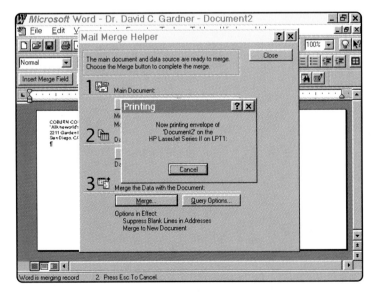

When the envelopes have printed, the Printing message box and the Mail Merge Helper dialog box will close.

The *unsaved* merge envelope screen will appear.

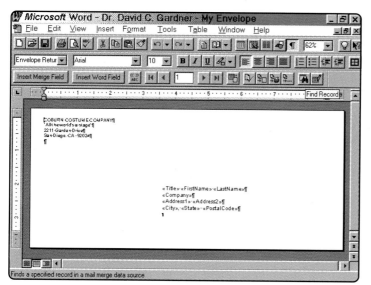

10. Repeat steps 1 through 3 in the section entitled "Saving the Label Document File" to name the envelope file "My Envelope" and save it.

PRINTING AN ENVELOPE FOR A SPECIFIC ADDRESS FROM A MAILING LIST

If you want to print an envelope for a specific address from your mailing list, you need to know the location of that address (record number) in the list before you can merge print. Word makes it easy to search for a specific name, address, postal code, etc.

Finding a Specific Address

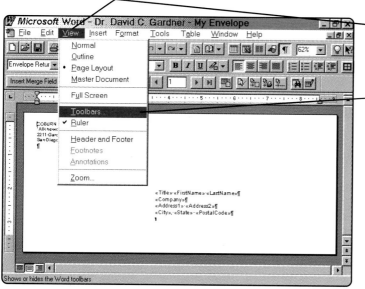

1. Click on **View** in the menu bar. The View menu will appear.

2. Click on **Toolbars**. The Toolbars dialog box will appear.

3. **Click** on **Database** to place a ✔ in the box.

4. **Click** on **OK**. The dialog box will close.

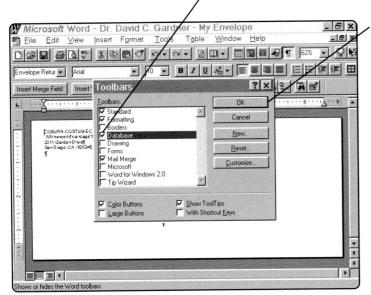

5. **Click** on the **Data Form tool** on the database toolbar. The Data Form dialog box will appear.

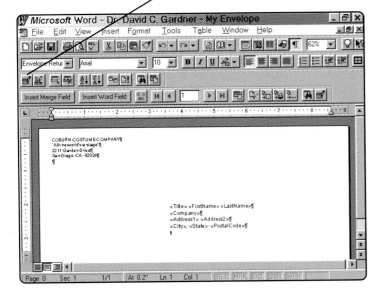

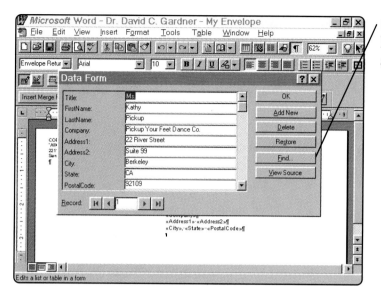

6. Click on **Find**. The Find In Field dialog box will appear.

7. Type Johnson in the Find What text box.

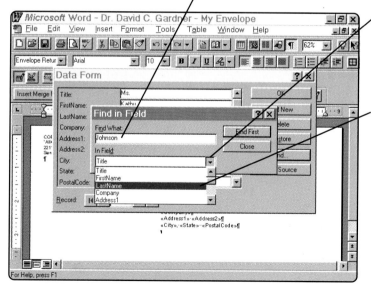

8. Click on the ▼ to the right of the In Field text box. A list of field names will appear.

9. Click on **LastName**. It will appear in the In Field text box.

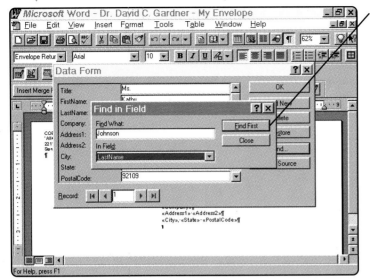

10. Click on **Find First**. Mr. Johnson's record number will appear in the Record box.

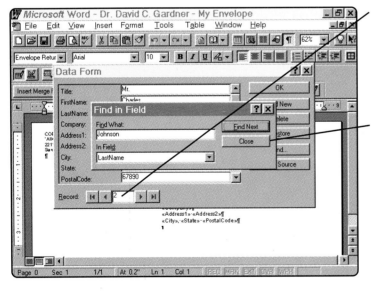

Notice that Mr. Johnson's record number is "2". You will need the record number to print an envelope just for him.

11. Click on **Close**. The Data Form dialog box will appear. Mr. Johnson's record will be shown.

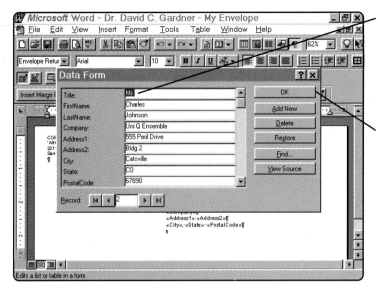

Notice that the Johnson data information appears in the Data Form dialog box. The record number "2" appears in the Record box.

12. **Click** on **OK**. The Data Form dialog box will close.

MERGE PRINTING
A SPECIFIC ENVELOPE

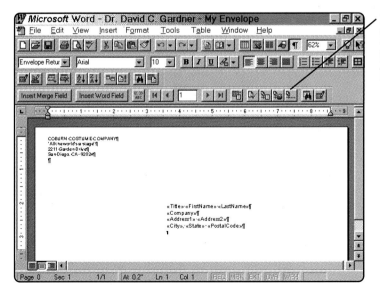

1. **Click** on the **Mail Merge button** on the mail merge toolbar. The Merge dialog box will appear.

2. **Click** on **From** to place a dot in the circle. The cursor will be flashing in the text box.

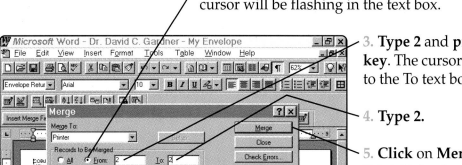

3. **Type 2** and **press** the **Tab key**. The cursor will move to the To text box.

4. **Type 2**.

5. **Click** on **Merge**. The Print dialog box will appear.

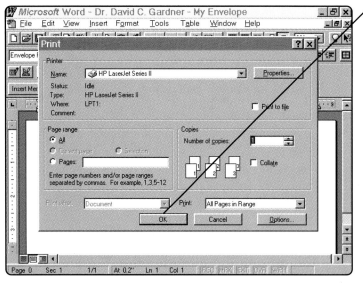

6. **Click** on **OK**. The envelope will print, and the Print dialog box will disappear.

REMOVING THE TOOLBAR

The database toolbar will remain on your screen until you remove it.

1. **Click** on **View** in the menu bar. The View menu will appear.

2. **Click** on **Toolbars**. The Toolbars dialog box will appear.

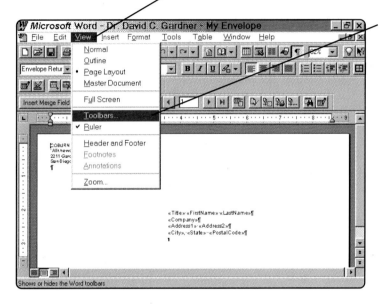

3. **Click** on **Database** to *remove* the ✔ from the box.

4. **Click** on **OK**. The dialog box will close, and the toolbar will be removed.

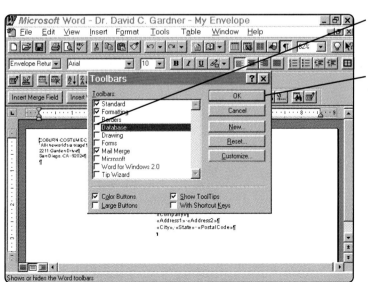

SAVING AND CLOSING THE DOCUMENT

1. **Click** on the **Save button** in the toolbar. The changes to My Envelope will be saved.

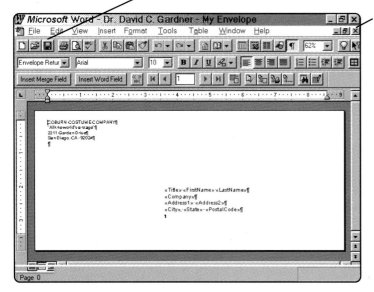

2. **Click** on the **Close button** on the menu bar. A Microsoft Word dialog box will appear.

Be careful not to click on the Close button on the title bar. This will close the entire program.

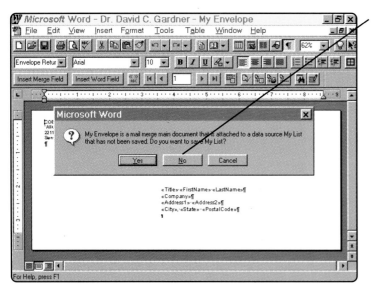

3. **Click** on **No**. Because you made no changes to My List, it's not necessary to save it at this time. However, if not saving a document makes you nervous, click on Yes.

WORD FOR WINDOWS 95

Part IV: Introducing Tables

Creating a Table and Using AutoFormat

The Tables feature in Word 7 makes it easy to organize information into columns and rows. You can join cells in the table to make room for a heading, increase the number of lines in a cell for a multiline entry, change the width of a column, and add and delete rows and columns with ease. You can also sort data on various criteria. Word has a selection of 34 different predesigned formats which you can apply to your table to create visual interest. In this chapter, you will do the following:

✔ Create a table
✔ Apply a predesigned AutoFormat to the table
✔ Join cells
✔ Enter and format text and numbers
✔ Align text and numbers within the table

CREATING A TABLE

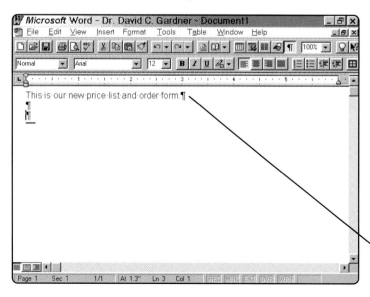

In this chapter you will create a table with four columns and six rows. You can insert a table anywhere in an existing document. In this example, however, you will open a new document for the table.

1. **Open** a **new document** if you haven't already done so.

2. **Type** the sentence **This is our new price list and order form.** Then **press Enter twice**.

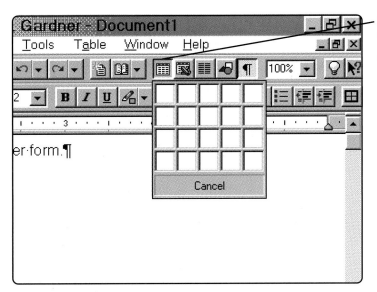

3. **Click** on the **Insert Table button** on the toolbar. A table grid will appear.

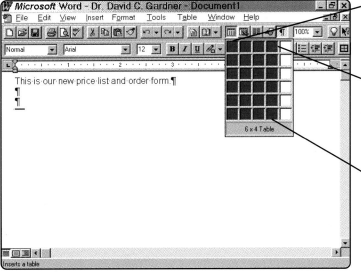

4. **Press and hold** on the **first square** of the table grid.

5. **Drag** the highlight bar **across four squares**. This tells Word to put four columns in the table.

6. **Continue to hold** the **mouse button** and **drag** the highlight bar **down six rows**. The grid will add two rows as you drag.

7. **Release** the **mouse button**. A six-row by four-column table will appear.

You can also create a table by clicking on Table in the menu bar then clicking on Insert Table on the pull-down menu. But it's not nearly as much fun as using the Insert Table button.

Notice the column indicators in the ruler bar.

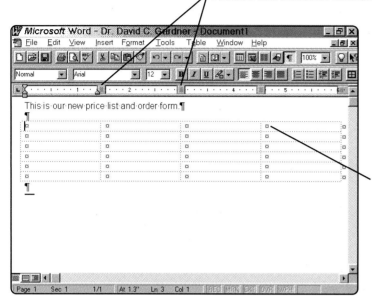

The columns are referred to as A through D. The rows are referred to as 1 through 6. The intersection of each column and row creates a cell. The cells are referred to as A1 through D6.

Notice also the gray squares in the table's cells. These are officially called "end-of-cell-marks" and act just like the ¶ marks in the document.

USING TABLE AUTOFORMAT

Word has 34 predesigned formats that you can apply to your table to give it a polished look.

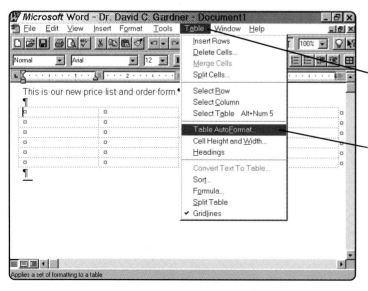

1. **Click** in the **first row** of the table to place the cursor.

2. **Click** on **Table** in the menu bar. The Table menu will appear.

3. **Click** on **Table AutoFormat.**The Table AutoFormat dialog box will appear.

Notice that the choice highlighted in the Formats list box is shown in the Preview box on the right.

Notice also that you can choose which features of the style you want by clicking the ✔ in each box on or off.

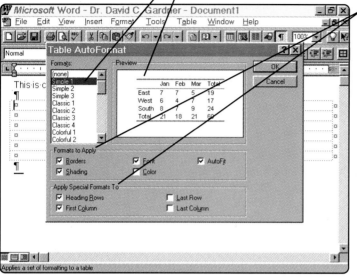

4. **Click** on the scroll bar to scroll through the list of formatting choices.

5. **Click** on **Colorful 2** when you have finished viewing all the choices.

6. **Click** on **OK**. The dialog box will close, and the table will appear with the Colorful 2 formatting.

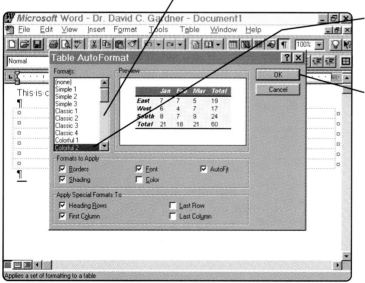

MERGING CELLS

When you merge cells, you remove the dividing lines between them to create a single, larger cell. In this section you will merge cells in the first row to create a single cell for a two-line heading.

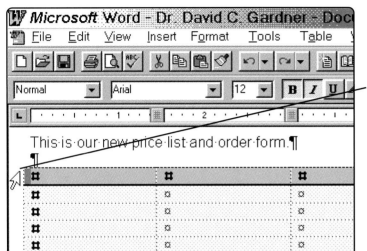

1. **Click** in the left margin **beside** the **first row**. The entire row will be highlighted.

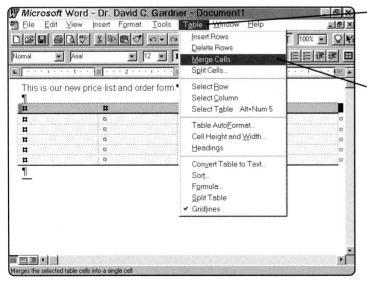

2. **Click** on **Table** in the menu bar. The Table menu will appear.

3. **Click** on **Merge Cells**. The dividing lines will be removed from the cells in the first row.

4. **Click anywhere** on the document to remove the highlighting and see the change.

ENTERING TEXT AND NUMBERS IN A TABLE

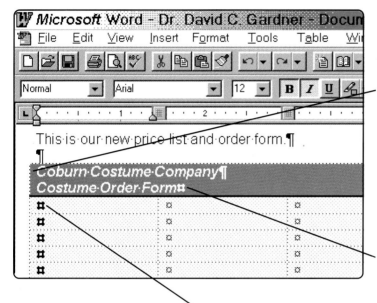

You enter and edit text in a table just as you do in the document itself.

1. **Click** in the **first row** in the table (Cell A1) if your cursor is not already there. **Type Coburn Costume Company**.

2. **Press Enter**. This will add a line to the cell you are in.

3. **Type Costume Order Form**.

4. **Press** the **Tab** key on your keyboard. This will move you to the next cell, A2.

5. **Type Costume** and **press** the **Tab** key. The cursor will move to the next cell (B2). If you accidentally press Enter, an extra line will be added to the cell. Simply press the Backspace key and the extra line will be deleted.

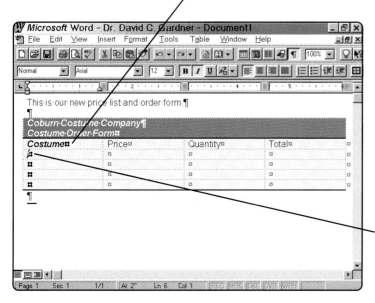

6. **Type Price** and **press Tab** to move to the next cell.

7. **Type Quantity** and **press Tab**. The cursor will move to the next cell.

8. **Type Total** and **press Tab**. The cursor will move to the first cell in the next row.

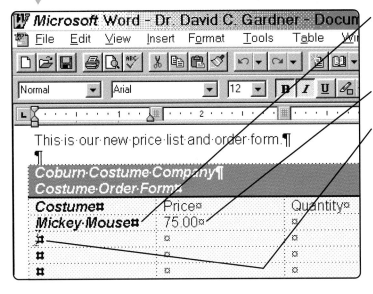

9. **Type Mickey Mouse** in C1, and **press Tab** to move the cursor to the next cell.

10. **Type 75.00**.

11. **Place** the **mouse pointer** inside the blank cell **below "Mickey Mouse"** just to the left of the gray square. The pointer will become an I-beam.

When you're in a table, the cursor changes shape with annoying speed. You may have to fiddle with the placement until you get the shape you want.

12. **Click** to set the cursor in place.

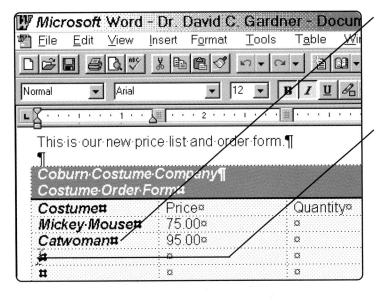

13. **Type Catwoman,** and **press Tab** to move to the next cell.

14. **Type 95.00**.

15. **Click** in the blank cell **below Catwoman**. (Remember that your cursor should be in the shape of an I-beam when you click in the cell.)

16. **Type Phantom Mask,** and **press Tab** to move to the next cell.

17. **Type 9.95**.

18. **Click** in the blank cell **below Phantom Mask** to place the cursor.

(You can move through the table with the Tab key, the arrow keys on your keyboard, or simply by clicking on the cell you want.)

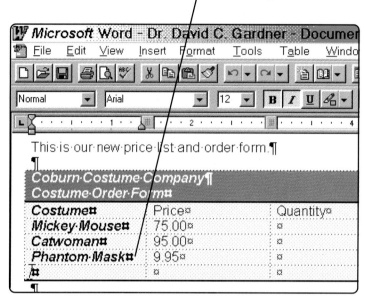

19. **Type Totals**.

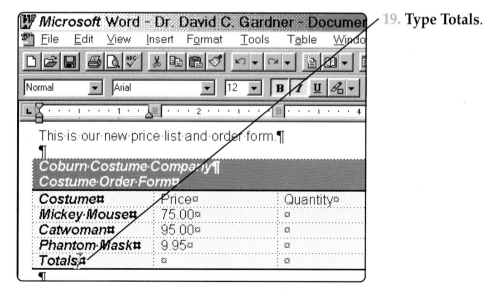

CENTERING TEXT IN A TABLE

You format the data in a table the same way you format it in the document itself. First, you highlight the text you want to format.

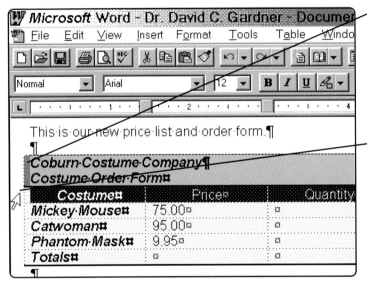

1. **Click** in the left margin **beside "Coburn Costume Company."** The entire row will be highlighted. (The mouse pointer should be in the shape of an arrow.)

2. **Press and hold** the **mouse button** and **drag** the arrow down to **Costume**. All three lines of type will be highlighted.

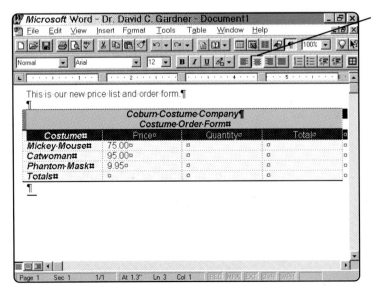

3. **Click** on the **Center button** on the toolbar. The highlighted text will be centered in each cell.

4. **Click anywhere** to remove the highlighting.

ALIGNING NUMBERS IN A TABLE

In this example you will align the numbers in column B to the right of the cell on the decimal point.

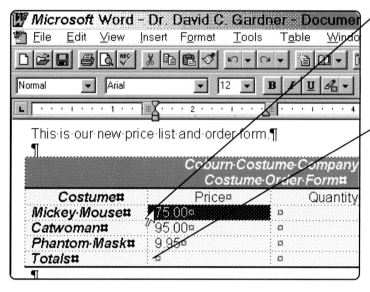

1. **Place** the **mouse pointer** in B3 just to the **left of 75**. It should be in the shape of a right-pointing arrow. **Click** to highlight the cell.

2. **Click and hold** the **mouse button** and **drag** the arrow down to B6. All four cells in column B will be highlighted.

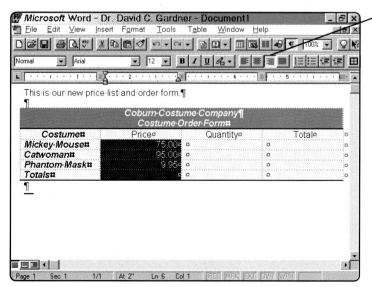

3. **Click** on the **Right-Align button** on the toolbar. The highlighted text will move to the right of the cell and line up on the decimal point.

4. **Click anywhere** to remove the highlighting.

SAVING THE TABLE

1. **Click** on the **Save button** on the toolbar. The Save As dialog box will appear as you see in this example.

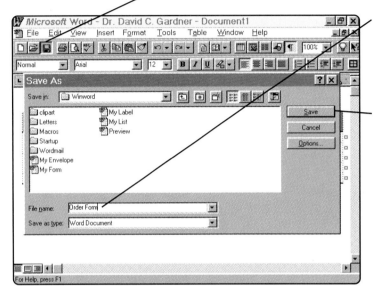

2. **Type Order Form**. It will replace the highlighted text that appears in the File name box.

3. **Click** on **Save**. The dialog box will close, and the table will be saved.

Editing a Table

You'll love the ease with which you can edit the contents of a table as well as change the structure of the table itself. You can sort data in a table (or in a letter) alphabetically and numerically. You can add and delete rows and columns with ease. You can also print a table with or without grid lines. In this chapter, you will do the following:

✔ Sort data alphabetically on the first cell in a row
✔ Sort data numerically on the second cell in a row
✔ Add and delete a row and a column
✔ Change column width
✔ Undo and redo multiple steps
✔ Change the position of a table so that it is centered across the page
✔ Print a table with or without grid lines
✔ Delete a table

SORTING DATA ALPHABETICALLY

You can sort data in a document and in a table. In this example you will sort the data in rows 3 through 5 alphabetically by the first cell in each row. Because you do not want to sort the entire table, you will highlight only the rows you want to sort.

1. **Click** outside the table **beside "Mickey Mouse."** The pointer will be in the shape of an arrow. The entire row will be highlighted.

2. **Press and hold** the **mouse button** as you **drag** the arrow down to the **Phantom Mask row**. All three rows will be highlighted.

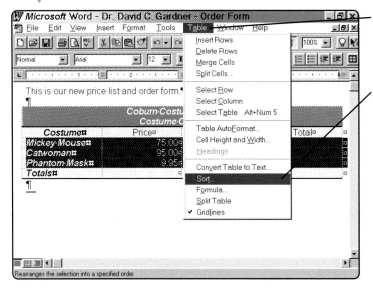

3. **Click** on **Table** in the menu bar. The Table menu will appear.

4. **Click** on **Sort**. The Sort dialog box will appear.

5. **Confirm** that **Column 1** is in the Sort By box. This means that the data will be sorted on the first cell in the row.

6. **Confirm** that **Text** is in the Type box. This means that data will be sorted alphabetically.

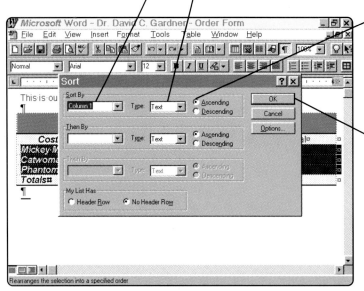

7. **Click** on **Ascending** to put a dot in the circle if one is not already there. *Ascending* means the sort will be in A to Z (or 1 to *n*) order.

8. **Click** on **OK**. The dialog box will close, and the highlighted lines will be sorted alphabetically based on the first cell in each row.

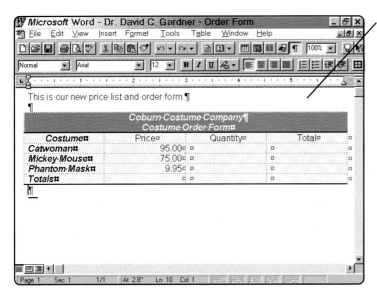

9. **Click anywhere** on the document to remove the highlighting.

Your screen will look like this example.

SORTING DATA NUMERICALLY

In this example you will sort the data in rows 3 through 5 based on the second cell in each row.

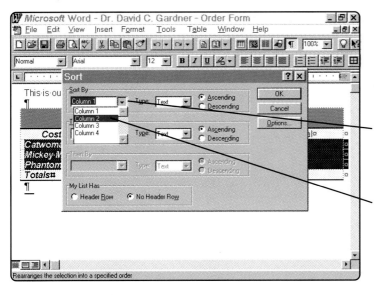

1. **Repeat steps 1 through 4** in the previous section to highlight rows 3 through 5 and to open the Sort dialog box.

2. **Click** on the ▼ to the right of Sort By. A pull-down list will appear.

3. **Click** on **Column 2**.

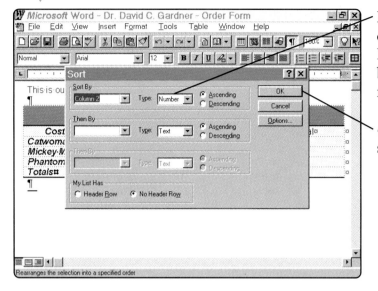

Notice that Word has changed the type to Number in the Type box because it knew there were numbers in column 2.

4. **Click** on **OK** to start the sorting process.

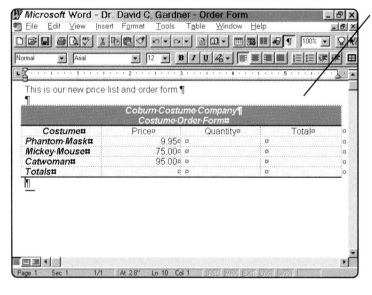

5. **Click anywhere** to remove the highlighting.

Your screen will look like this.

UNDOING A SORT

You can undo a sort with the click of your mouse. But be sure *not to perform any other function* between the numeric sort and the Undo or else it won't work. In this example, you will undo the numeric sort you just applied in the previous section and return to the alphabetic sort.

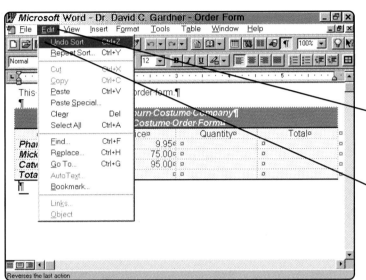

1. **Click** on **Edit** in the menu bar. The Edit menu will appear.

2. **Click** on **Undo Sort**.

ADDING A ROW

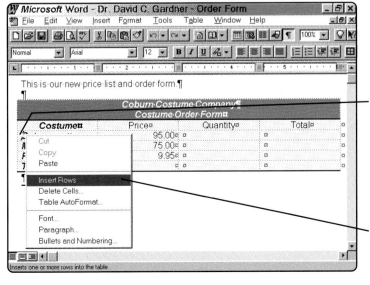

You can add a row anywhere in the table. In this example you will add a row above row 3.

1. **Click** on **"Catwoman"** in row 3 to place the cursor.

2. **Click** the **right mouse button**. A quick menu will appear.

3. **Click** on **Insert Rows**. A row will be added to the table above row 3.

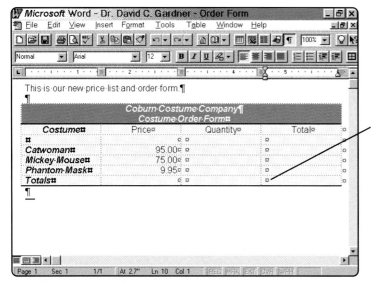

If you think adding a row in the middle of a table was easy, wait until you see how easily you can add a row to the end of a table.

4. **Click** in the **last cell** of the table to place the cursor.

5. **Press** the **Tab key**. Another row will be added to the end of the table. (Remember, if you press the Enter key you will increase the height of the current row.)

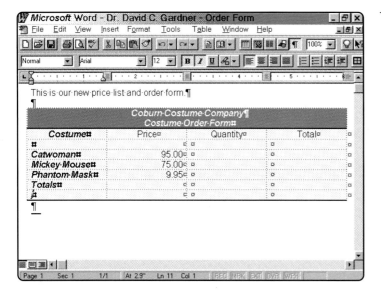

Your table will look like this.

DELETING A ROW

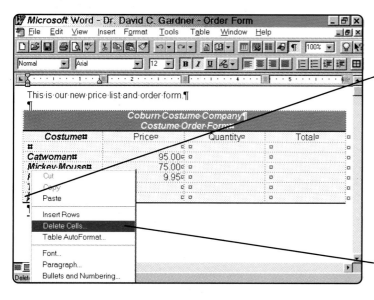

You can delete a row as easily as you added one.

1. **Click** in the row you want to delete. In this example, click in the **last row** if your cursor is not already there.

2. **Click** the **right mouse button**. A quick menu will appear.

3. **Click** on **Delete Cells**. The Delete Cells dialog box will appear.

4. **Click** on **Delete Entire Row** to insert a dot in the circle. (To delete the column where the cursor is placed you would click on Delete Entire Column.)

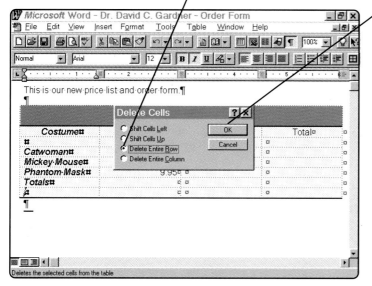

5. **Click** on **OK**. The row will be deleted.

ADDING A COLUMN

Word will add a column to the left of a selected column. First, you have to highlight the entire column.

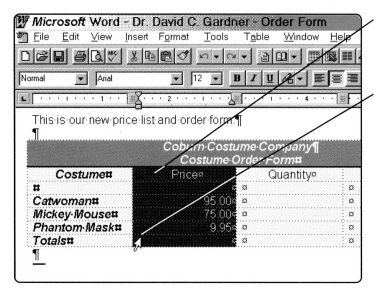

1. **Position** the **mouse pointer** in the **"Price" cell** so that it is an arrow.

2. **Press and hold** the **mouse button** and **drag** the arrow and the highlight bar down to the **last row** in column B.

3. **Keep** the **pointer** in the highlighted area, and **press** the *right* **mouse button**. A quick menu will appear.

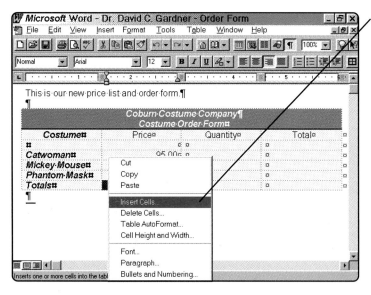

4. **Click** on **Insert Cells**. The Insert Cells dialog box will appear.

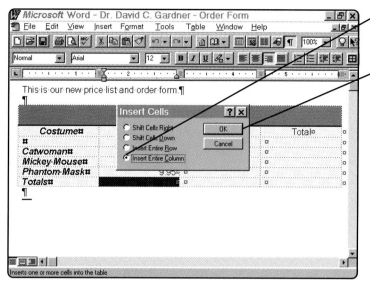

5. **Click** on **Insert Entire Column**.

6. **Click** on **OK**. A column the width of the highlighted column will be inserted to the left. The new column will contain the same formatting that was applied to the highlighted column. For example, the new cell B2 will center whatever you enter into the cell. You can, of course, change the formatting.

7. **Click** on the **Undo button** to remove the new column.

8. **Click anywhere** to remove the highlighting.

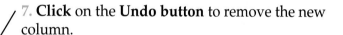

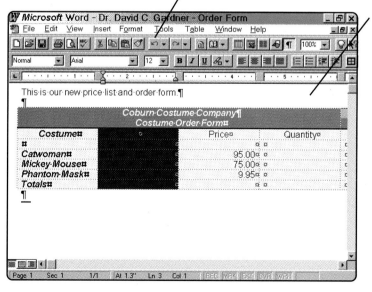

CHANGING COLUMN WIDTH

There are several ways to change the width of your columns. In the following section you will use two different methods to change the width of a column.

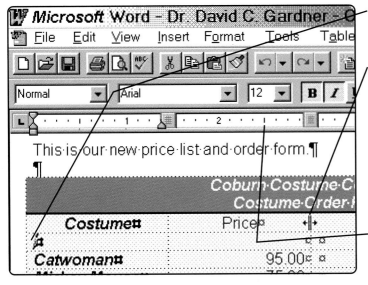

1. **Click** in **any column** in the table.

2. **Place** the **mouse arrow** on **top** of the **right boundary line** for column A so that your mouse pointer turns into the symbol you see here. You will probably have to fiddle with the cursor to get it into the right shape.

3. **Press and hold** the **mouse button** and **drag** the dotted line to the **2.5 inch mark** on the ruler bar. Then **release** the **mouse button**. The second column will now be 1 inch wide.

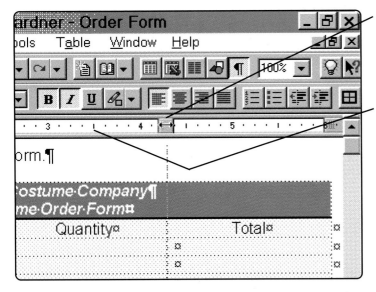

4. **Place** the **mouse arrow** on **top** of the **column 3 (C) column marker**. Your pointer will turn into a double arrow.

5. **Press and hold** the **mouse button** and **drag** the column marker to the **3.5 inch mark** on the ruler bar. Then **release** the **mouse button**. The third column will now be 1 inch wide.

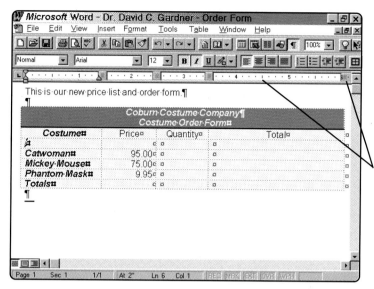

Notice that the table has remained the same overall size, and only the widths of columns B and C have changed. Now you will adjust the right edge of the table and change its size.

6. Use one of the **methods just shown** and **drag** the **right table boundary line** to the **4.5 inch mark** on the ruler bar.

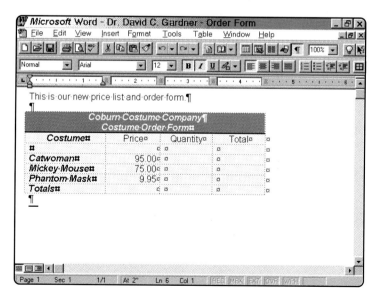

Your table will look like this example.

UNDOING AND REDOING MULTIPLE STEPS

Word keeps track of the changes you make. You can use the Multiple Undo feature to undo more than twenty previous steps! In this example you will undo the three changes you just made to column widths.

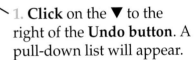

1. Click on the ▼ to the right of the **Undo button**. A pull-down list will appear.

2. Click and hold on the **first Column Width** and **drag** the highlight bar down to the **third Column Width**. When you **release** the **mouse button** the list will disappear, and the last three column width changes you made will be undone.

You can even redo a multiple undo! (Don't you wish life was so forgiving.)

3. Click on the ▼ to the right of the **Redo button**. A pull-down list will appear.

4. Click on the **first Column Width** and **drag** the highlight bar down to the **third Column Width**. Then **release** the **mouse button** to redo the width changes.

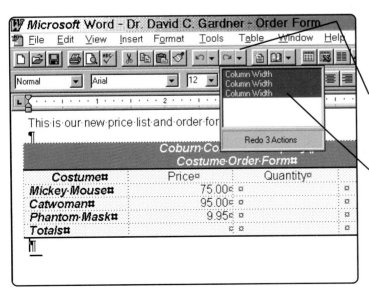

CENTERING THE TABLE

When Word first creates a table, it extends the table the width of the page. When you change column width Word keeps the same left margin. This often means that the table is no longer centered across the page. But you can center it very easily.

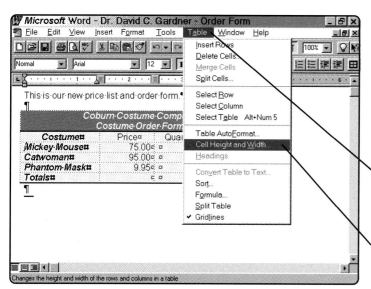

1. **Click anywhere** in the table if your cursor is not already there.

2. **Click** on **Table** in the menu bar. The Table menu will appear.

3. **Click** on **Cell Height and Width**. The Cell Height and Width dialog box will appear.

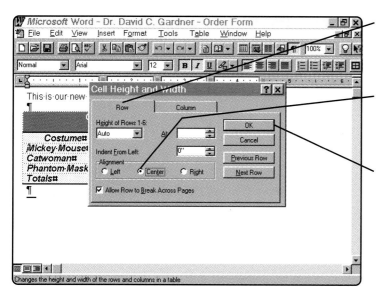

4. **Click** on the **Row tab** to bring the Row dialog box into view, if necessary.

5. **Click** on **Center** under Alignment to insert a dot into the circle.

6. **Click** on **OK**. The dialog box will close, and your table will now be centered across the page.

Your document will look like this example.

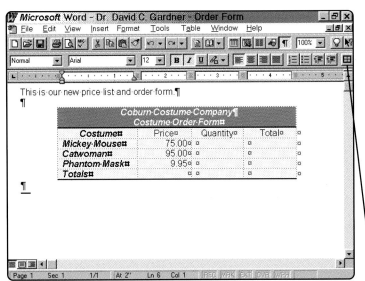

ADDING GRIDLINES FOR PRINTING

The gridlines you see on the screen will not print. If you want gridlines on the printed document, you have to add them.

1. Click on the **Borders button** on the toolbar. The border toolbar will appear on your screen.

Now you have to select the entire table in order to apply inside and outside border lines.

2. Click anywhere in the table to place the cursor.

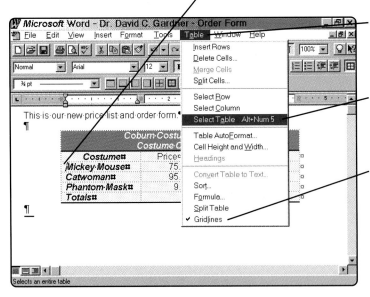

3. Click on **Table** in the menu bar. The Table list will appear.

4. Click on **Select Table**. The entire table will be highlighted.

The ✔ next to Gridlines means that gridlines show on the screen. It has nothing to do with the printed page. Clicking on Gridlines would remove the ✔ and the gridlines would not show on the screen.

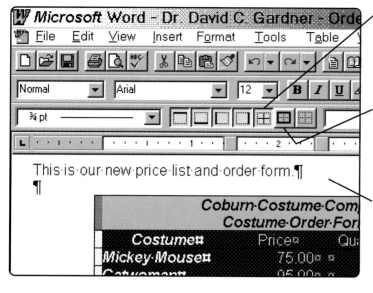

5. **Click** on the **Inside Border button** on the border toolbar to put lines inside the table.

6. **Click** on the **Outside Border button** on the border toolbar to put lines on the outside of the table.

7. **Click anywhere** to remove the highlighting and see the lines.

REMOVING THE LINES FROM THE PRINTED PAGE

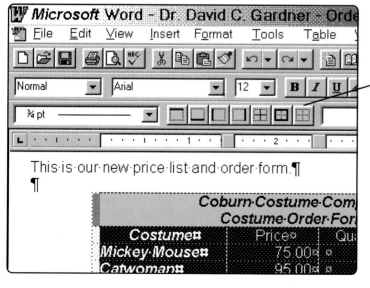

1. **Repeat steps 2 through 4** in the previous section to select the entire table.

2. **Click** on the **No Border button** on the border toolbar to remove the inside and outside lines.

3. **Click anywhere** to remove the highlighting.

DELETING AND UNDELETING A TABLE

Deleting and undeleting a table is as easy as deleting and undeleting text. In this example, you will delete the table in the Order Form document.

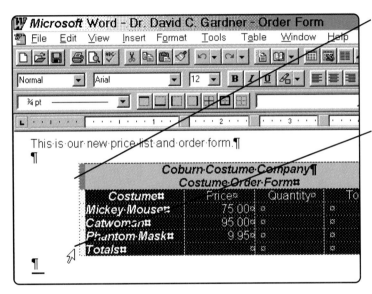

1. **Click** outside the table **next to** the **first line**. The cursor will be in the shape of an arrow. The line will be highlighted.

2. **Press and hold** the **mouse button** and **drag** the arrow down to the end of the table. The entire table will be highlighted. (This is another way to select the entire table.)

3. **Click** on the **Cut button** on the toolbar. The table will be deleted from the document.

4. **Click** on the **Undo button** to restore the table to your screen.

5. **Click** on the **Borders button** on the toolbar to remove the borders toolbar.

6. **Click** on the **Save button**.

7. **Click** on the **Close Document button**.

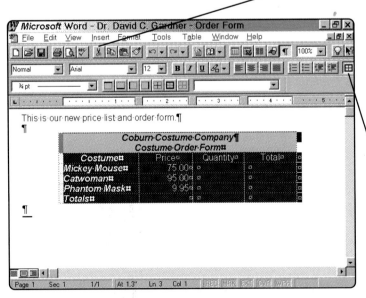

WORD FOR WINDOWS 95

Part V: Working Smarter

Using the
Wizard Template

A template is a predesigned form for a letter, memo, report, or other word processing document that you use over and over again. A Wizard template allows you to enter text into the form with a series of dialog boxes. In Chapter 20, you will customize a standard template. In this chapter, you will do the following:

✔ Set up a Wizard template
✔ Print a Wizard product

SELECTING A WIZARD TEMPLATE

1. **Click** on **File.** The File menu will appear.

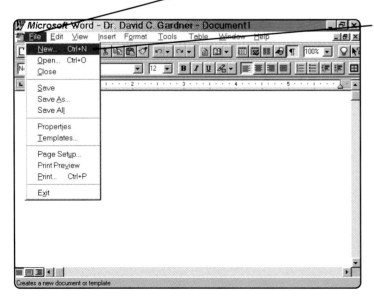

2. **Click** on **New.** The New dialog box will appear. It will show the icons for the standard and Wizard templates.

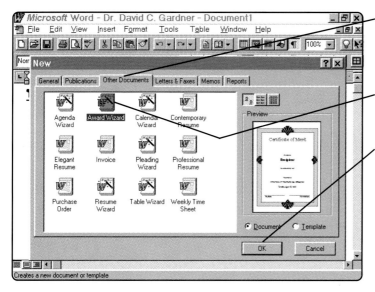

3. **Click** on the **Other Documents tab** to bring it to the front.

4. **Click** on **Award Wizard**. It will be highlighted.

5. **Click** on **OK**. There will be a fairly long hourglass intermission. Then, the Award Wizard dialog box will appear.

FILLING IN THE TEXT

Notice that there are four award layout options. You can view them in this dialog box by clicking on the circle next to the option. The certificate will appear in the preview box.

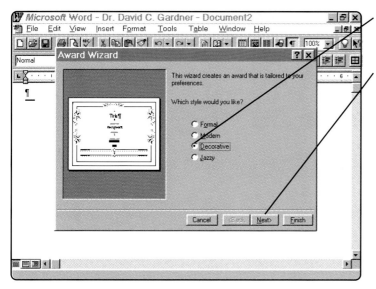

1. **Click** on **Decorative** to place a dot in the circle.

2. **Click** on **Next>**. A new Award Wizard dialog box will appear.

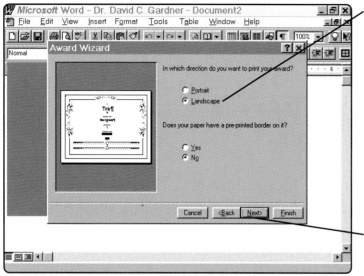

Notice that Landscape printing (also known as sideways printing) is selected. This means that the printing will be done with the long side of the paper at the top. If you choose portrait orientation (which is how most letters are normally printed) the short side of the paper is at the top.

3. **Click** on **Next>**. Another Award Wizard dialog box will appear.

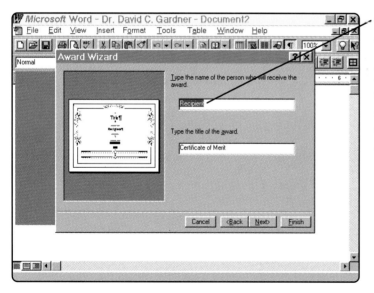

4. **Click twice** on "**Recipient**" to highlight it.

Note: If there's more than one word in the text box, click at the end of the last word, then drag to the left to highlight all the words.

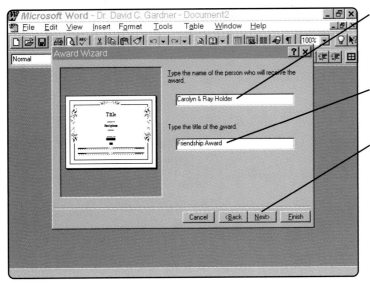

5. **Type** the **name** of the person(s) receiving the award.

6. **Repeat steps 4 and 5** to fill in the title of the award.

7. **Click** on **Next>**. Another Award Wizard dialog box will appear.

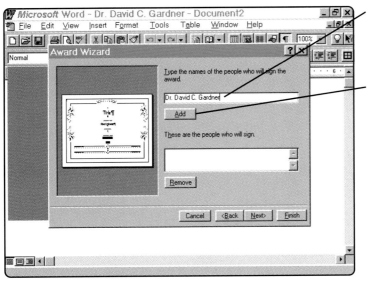

8. **Repeat steps 4 and 5** to type the name of the first person signing the award.

9. **Click** on **Add**. The typed name will move to the text box below.

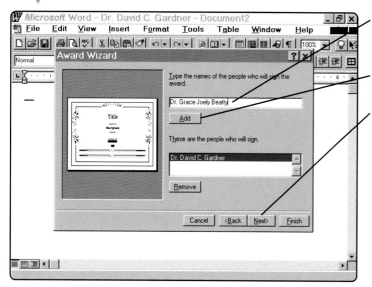

10. **Type** the **name** of the second signer of the award.

11. **Click** on **Add**.

12. **Click** on **Next>**.

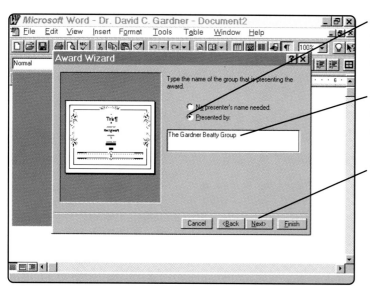

13. **Click** on the **circle** to the **left** of **Presented by** to place a dot in it.

14. **Repeat steps 4 and 5** to type the name of the group that is presenting the award.

15. **Click** on **Next>**.

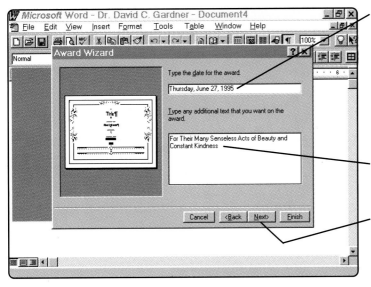

Notice that the current date is automatically selected in the text box.

16. **Repeat steps 4 and 5** if you want to change the date. If not, go to step 17.

17. **Repeat steps 4 and 5** to type any additional text.

18. **Click** on **Next>**.

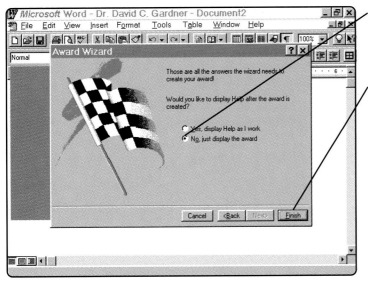

19. **Click** on the **circle** next to No to put a dot in it, if necessary.

20. **Click** on **Finish**. After a brief hourglass intermission, the complete certificate will appear on your screen. Wow!

PREVIEWING THE WIZARD PRODUCT

1. **Click** on **File** in the menu bar. The File menu will appear.

2. **Click** on **Print Preview**.

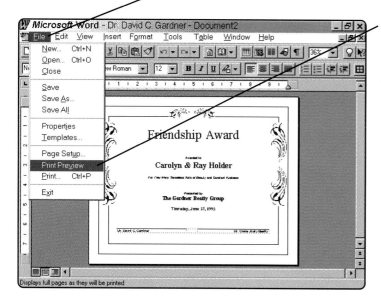

PRINTING THE WIZARD PRODUCT

1. **Click** on the **Print button** in the toolbar. After awhile, the certificate will print.

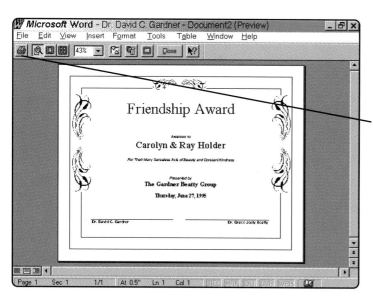

CLOSING THE WIZARD TEMPLATE

1. **Click** on **File** in the menu bar. The File menu will appear.

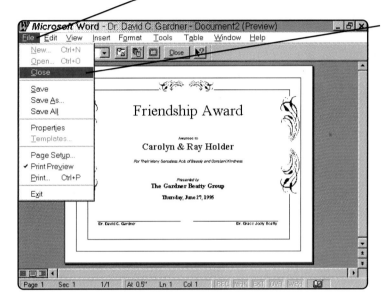

2. **Click** on **Close**. A Microsoft Word dialog box will appear.

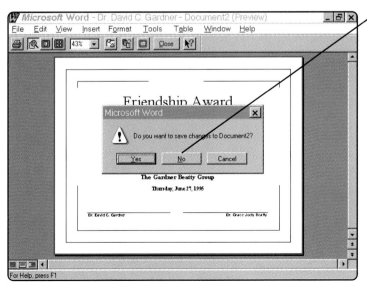

3. **Click** on **No**. If you need to revise this certificate, Award Wizard will automatically come up in the same format the next time you select it. You will need to open Award Wizard again, then click on Next until you find the screen that you want to change.

You now are ready to go on to the next chapter.

Making a
Customized Template

You learned how to use a standard Wizard template in Chapter 19. In this chapter, you'll learn how to customize a Wizard template by adding a logo to the memo template and changing the text. In this chapter, you will do the following:

✔ Create a new template by using Save As
✔ Add a graphic to a template
✔ Customize the text

OPENING A
STANDARD TEMPLATE

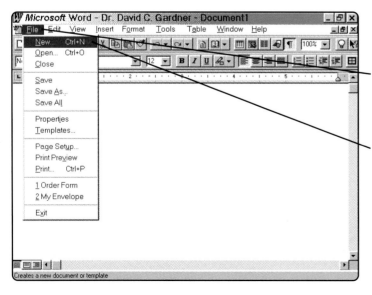

1. **Open** a **new document** if one is not already open.

2. **Click** on **File** in the menu bar. A pull-down menu will appear.

3. **Click** on **New**. The New dialog box will appear.

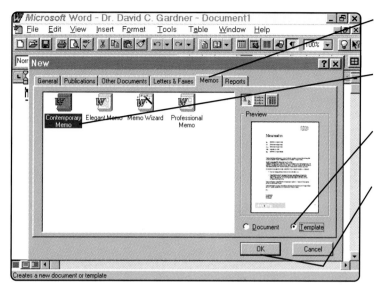

4. **Click** on the **Memos tab** to bring it to the front.

5. **Click** on **Contemporary Memo** to highlight it.

6. **Click** on **Template** to put a dot in the circle.

7. **Click** on **OK**. Template1 will appear on your screen in Page Layout view.

SAVING THE FILE AS A NEW TEMPLATE

1. **Click** on **File** in the menu bar. A pull-down menu will appear.

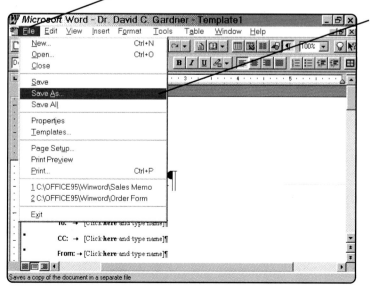

2. **Click** on **Save As**. The Save As dialog box will appear.

Notice that the Templates folder shows in the Save in text box.

3. **Type Sales Memo** in the File name text box. It will replace the highlighted text.

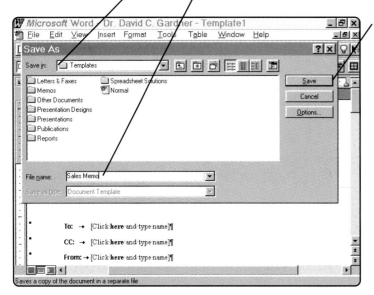

4. **Click** on **Save**. The file will be saved as the Sales Memo.dot template in the Templates folder.

You are now ready to modify the new template. (The original template has not changed.)

ADDING A GRAPHIC TO THE TEMPLATE

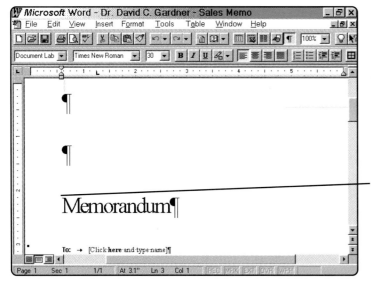

Notice that the cursor is flashing before the word Memorandum.

1. **Press** the **Enter key twice** to move the word Memorandum down two lines to make room for a graphic.

2. **Press** the ↑ on your keyboard twice to move the cursor up two lines.

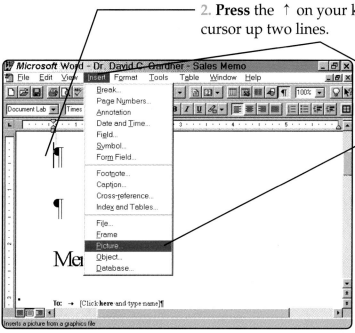

3. **Click** on **Insert** in the menu bar. A pull-down menu will appear.

4. **Click** on **Picture**. The Insert Picture dialog box will appear.

5. **Click** on the **Preview button** to see the pictures, if necessary.

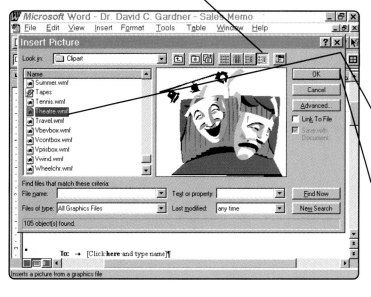

6. **Click repeatedly** on the ▼ to the right of the Name list box to scroll down the list.

7. **Click** on **Theatre.wmf**. It will move to the File name list box.

8. **Click** on **OK**. The theatre picture will appear on your screen.

Changing the View

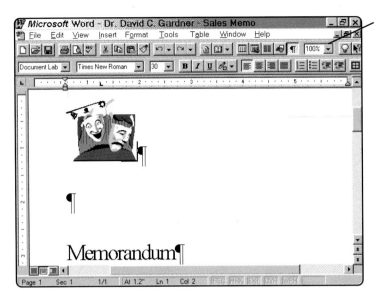

1. **Click** on the **Zoom control** ▼. A pull-down list will appear.

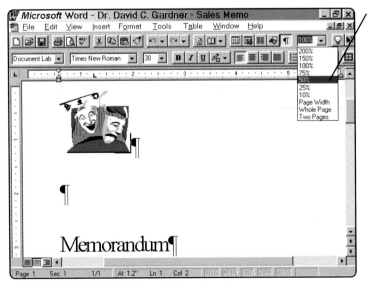

2. **Click** on **50%.** The picture (Theatre.wmf) can now be viewed more easily in relation to the text.

Sizing the Graphic

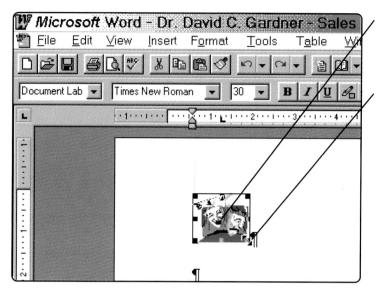

1. **Click** on the **graphic**. It will be surrounded by a black border with handles.

2. **Place** the **mouse arrow** on the **lower right corner**. It will turn into a two-headed arrow.

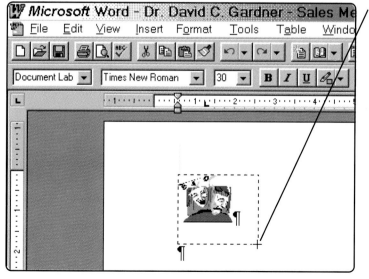

3. **Press and hold** the **mouse arrow** as you **move** it down and to the right. A dotted box will appear. It represents the "new" size of the graphic as you size it.

4. **Release** the **mouse button** when you think the new size is about right. You may have to fiddle with it to get it the way you want.

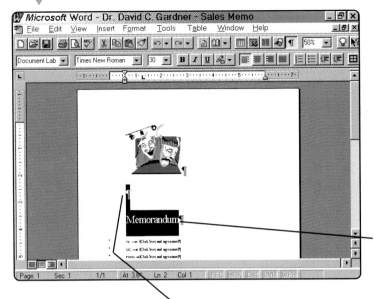

CUSTOMIZING TEXT

You can remove, reposition, replace, or change any or all of the elements that make up a template. An element is a graphic or a section of text. In this example, we'll change the font size.

1. **Click** at the end of **"Memorandum"** to place the cursor between the word and the ¶ symbol.

2. **Drag** the **cursor** up to the **first ¶ symbol**. Both lines will be highlighted.

3. **Click** on the ▼ to the right of the font size box. A pull-down menu will appear.

4. **Click repeatedly** on the ▲ on the scroll bar to bring 18 into view.

5. **Click** on **18**. The menu will close, and both lines of highlighted text will change to 18 points.

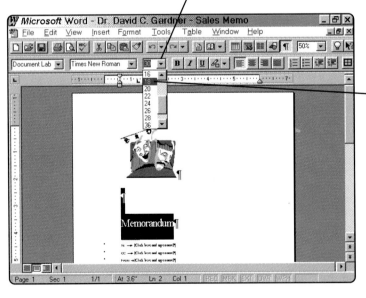

ENTERING BOILERPLATE TEXT

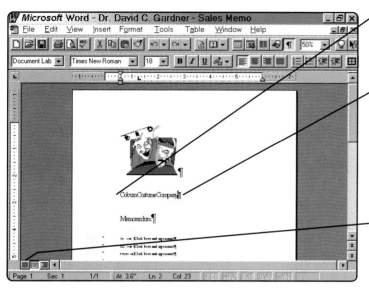

1. **Click** the **mouse arrow** to the **left** of **the** ¶ below the graphic to set the cursor.

2. **Type Coburn Costume Company.** Notice that the type style is automatically the same as "Memorandum" (Times New Roman, 18pts, Bold).

3. **Click** on the **Normal View button** to return to the faster text editing mode.

4. **Click repeatedly** on the ▼ on the scroll bar to make your screen look similar to the example below.

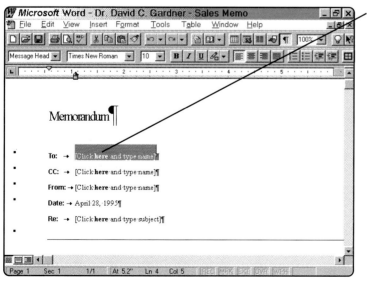

5. **Click** on **"here"** to highlight the line of text.

6. **Type West Coast Sales Group**.

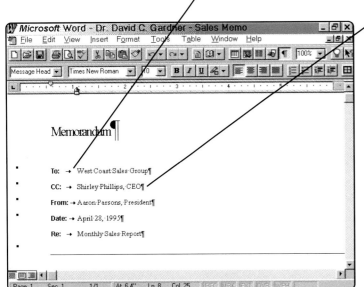

7. **Repeat steps 5 and 6 to type** the following:

Shirley Phillips, CEO

Aaron Parsons, President

Monthly Sales Report

SAVING AND CLOSING THE TEMPLATE

1. **Click** on the **Save button** in the toolbar.

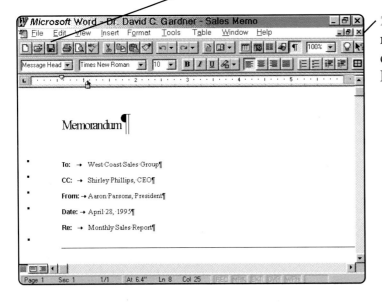

2. **Click** on the **Close Document button** ☒ to the right of the menu bar. Sales Memo will close.

Using AutoCorrect and AutoText

Most people have text or graphics that they use over and over again. Word has two ways you can store these frequently used items so that you can insert them into your document quickly. The first is AutoText, which allows you to insert a word or phrase or graphic into your document by typing a few key strokes, clicking a button, or using a command. AutoCorrect allows you to change an item as you type without clicking a button or using a command. In this chapter, you will do the following:

✔ Set up and use an AutoText entry
✔ Set up and use an AutoCorrect entry

USING AUTOTEXT

AutoText is an excellent program for storing and inserting text and graphics that you use frequently, such as the closing to a letter. You may also want to use AutoText for items that you want to insert automatically as you type.

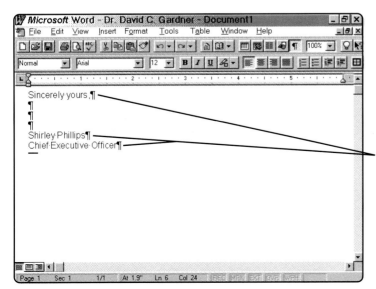

Open a new document if you haven't done so already.

Creating an AutoText Entry

1. **Type** a **closing** that you use for your letters. In this example we used a closing for Shirley Phillips, Chief Executive Officer.

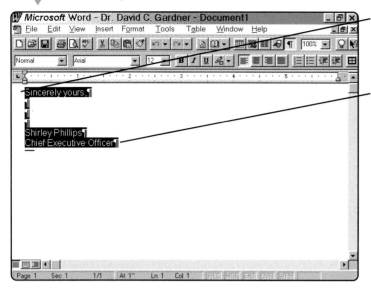

2. Click to the **left** of the "**S**" in "Sincerely" to place the cursor.

3. Press and hold the **mouse button** as you **drag** it down and to the right to highlight the text.

Notice that the style is Normal, the font is Arial, and the font size is 12.

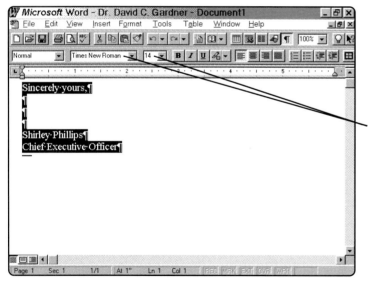

In this example, you'll change the text formatting so that you can see how the Insert As option in AutoText works.

4. Change the **font** to **Times New Roman**, and the **font size** to **14 pt.** If you need help with this, go to Chapter 1, "Changing Margins and Fonts and Entering Text."

5. **Click** on **Edit** in the menu bar. A pull-down menu will appear.

6. **Click** on **AutoText**. The AutoText dialog box will appear.

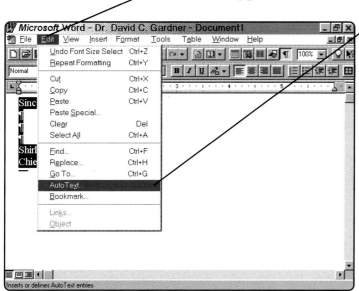

7. **Type closing.** It will replace the highlighted "Sincerely yours," in the Name text box.

8. **Click** on **Add**. "Closing" will move to the list of AutoText items. The dialog box will close.

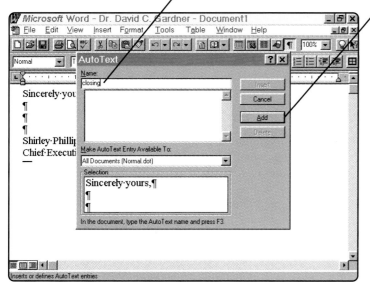

Inserting an AutoText Item with Different Formatting

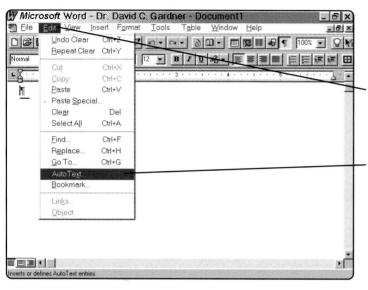

1. **Press** the **Delete key** to remove the highlighted text from the document.

2. **Click** on **Edit** in the Menu bar. The Edit menu will appear.

3. **Click** on **AutoText**. The AutoText dialog box will appear.

4. **Click** on **closing** to highlight it, if necessary. "Closing" will appear in the Name text box.

Notice that there is a dot in the circle to the left of Formatted Text.

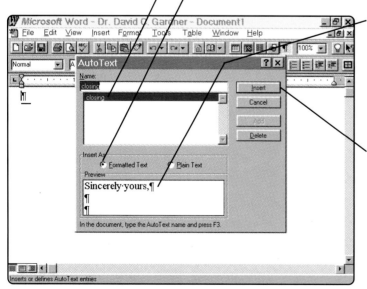

Notice also that "Sincerely yours," shows in the Preview box with the different formatting you gave it previously (14 pt. Times New Roman).

5. **Click** on **Insert**. The dialog box will disappear. The "closing" text, with the different formatting, will appear on the document.

Slick!

Inserting an AutoText Item with Plain Formatting

1. **Press Enter** to move the cursor down one line.

2. **Repeat steps 2 through 4** in the previous section to highlight "closing" in the AutoText dialog box.

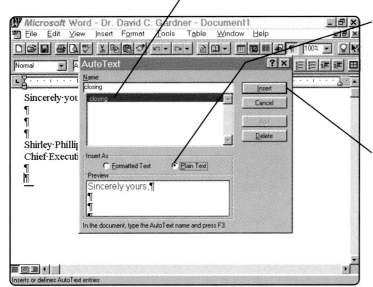

3. **Click** on **Plain Text** to place a dot in the circle.

Notice that "Sincerely yours," in the Preview box has changed formatting.

4. **Click** on **Insert**.

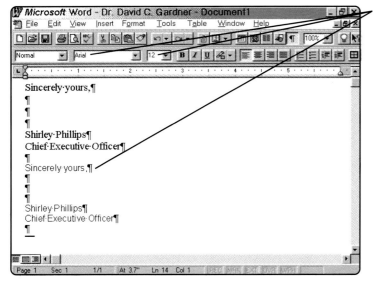

Notice that the formatting of the closing has changed to the same (standard) formatting as the document (12 pt. Arial).

CREATING AN AUTOCORRECT ENTRY

AutoCorrect is preprogrammed to automatically correct nine common typing errors and replace 3 preset entries with common symbols. In this example, you'll create an entry that will replace "asap" with the phrase "as soon as possible."

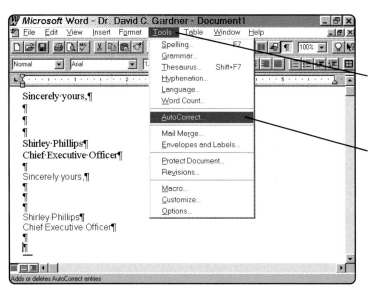

1. **Press** the **Enter key** to insert one line.

2. **Click** on **Tools** in the menu bar. A pull-down menu will appear.

3. **Click** on **AutoCorrect**. The AutoCorrect dialog box will appear.

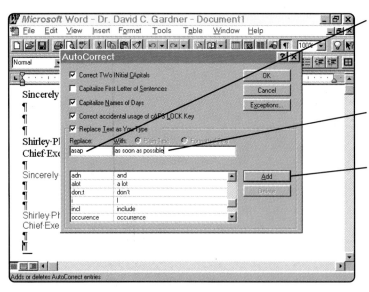

4. **Type asap** in the Replace text box.

5. **Press** the **Tab key**.

6. **Type as soon as possible** in the With text box.

7. **Click** on **Add**.

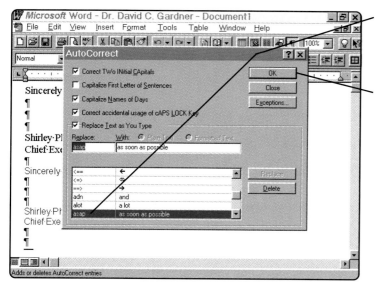

Notice that the text "asap" and the text to replace it are highlighted.

8. **Click** on **OK**. The dialog box will close.

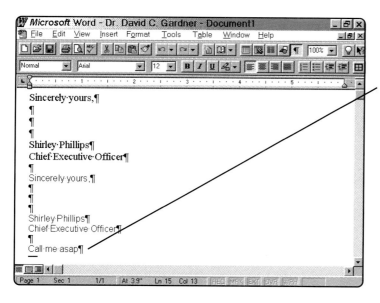

Inserting An AutoCorrect Item

1. **Type Call me asap.**

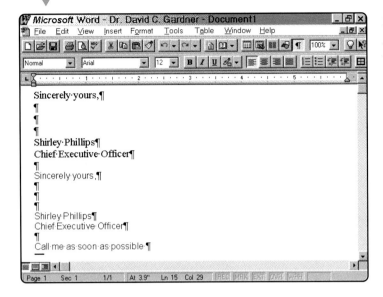

2. Press the **Spacebar once**. Zap! "Asap" is replaced by the new text.

CLOSING DOCUMENT1

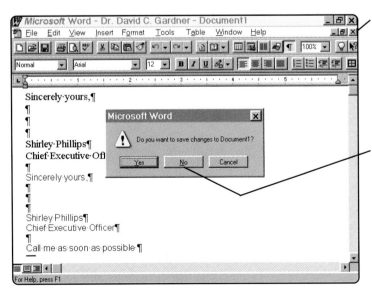

1. Click on the **Close Document button** on the menu bar. A Microsoft Word dialog box will appear, asking if you want to save changes to your document.

2. Click on **No.**

Creating a Macro

Creating a macro is a way to consolidate a series of commands into a single command. Carefully thought out macros can make everyday word processing tasks easier and faster. In Word 7, you can assign a macro to a menu, a toolbar, or shortcut keys. In this chapter, you will do the following:

✔ Open the Macro Recorder
✔ Assign the macro command to the File menu bar
✔ Record the macro
✔ Use the macro
✔ Delete the macro

SETTING UP THE MACRO

In this example you will create a simple macro. We urge you to go through these steps as a trial run before creating your own customized macro. It is very important to plan ahead when creating your own macros to avoid panicsville.

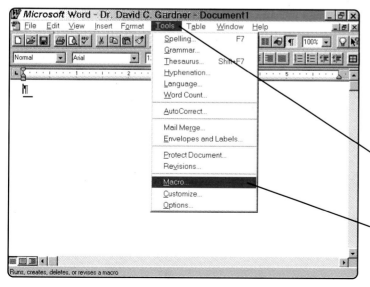

Open a new document if you haven't done so already.

Opening the Macro Recorder

1. **Click** on **Tools** in the menu bar. The Tools menu will appear.

2. **Click** on **Macro**. The Macro dialog box will appear.

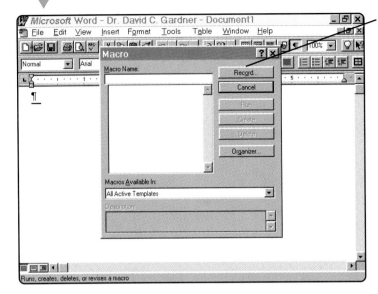

3. Click on **Record.** The Record Macro dialog box will appear. Macro1 will be highlighted in the Record Macro Name text box.

ASSIGNING THE MACRO COMMAND LOCATION

In this example, you'll tell Word to place your new macro command on the File menu, below the Open command.

1. Click in the **Description text box** to place the cursor.

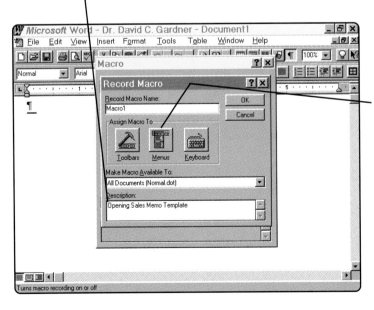

2. Type Opening Sales Memo Template in the Description text box.

3. Click on the **Menus button** in the Assign Macro To box. The Customize dialog box will appear.

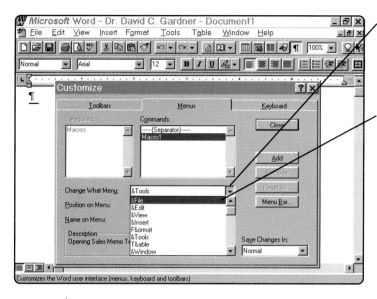

4. **Click** on the ▼ to the right of the Change What Menu list box. A pull-down list will appear.

5. **Click** on the menu option **&File**. The "&File" menu option will appear highlighted in the Change What Menu list box.

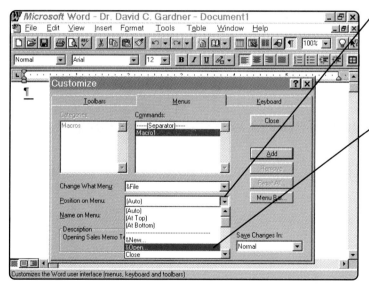

6. **Click** on the ▼ to the right of the Position on Menu list box. A pull-down list of menu locations will appear.

7. **Click** on the menu option **&Open**. The menu option "&Open"will appear in the Position on Menu list box.

8. **Press Tab**. The menu option "&Macro1," in the Name on Menu text box, will be highlighted.

9. **Type Open Sales Memo** in the Name on Menu box.

10. **Click** on **Add Below**. Open Sales Memo will appear in the Position on Menu list box.

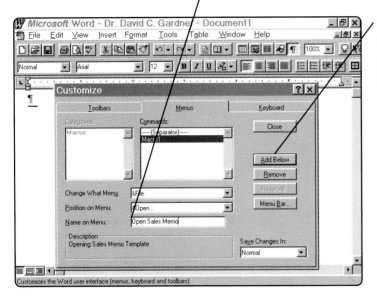

RECORDING THE MACRO

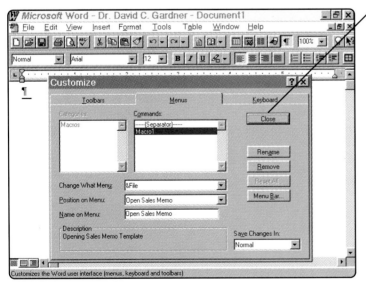

1. **Click** on **Close**. The dialog box will close, and the Document1 screen will appear.

Note: From this point on, everything you do will become part of your macro.

Notice the Macro Record toolbar.

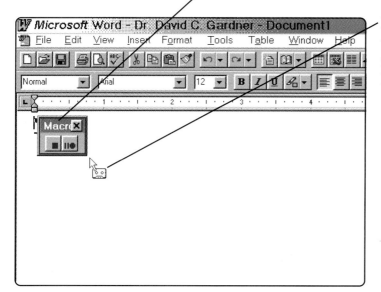

Notice the mouse pointer with the record graphic. It may appear in a different location on your screen.

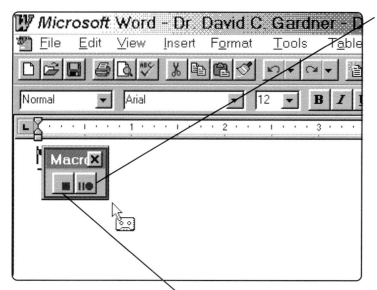

Notice that you can temporarily stop the recording process by clicking on the pause button on the right side of the toolbar. The Pause button allows you to move around the document and make any keystrokes without making them a part of the macro. When you are ready to record the macro again, click on the Pause button.

Warning: Do not click on the Stop button (left) on the toolbar until you have finished recording all of the steps you want in the macro. Once you click on the Stop button, the macro is completed and you may be macroed for life!

2. **Click** on **File** in the menu bar. The File menu will appear.

Notice that the new macro command, "Open Sales Memo," appears on the menu under the Open command. However, the macro is *not* complete until you finish the steps and click on the stop button.

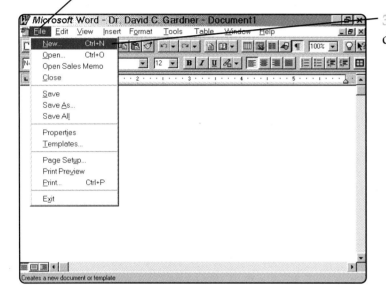

3. **Click** on **New**. The New dialog box will appear.

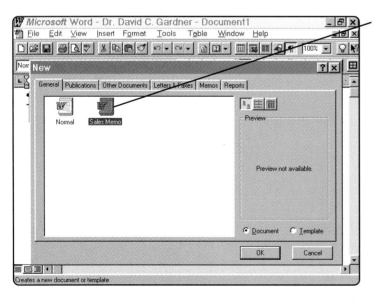

4. **Click twice** on **Sales Memo**. The Sales Memo document will appear on the screen as Document2.

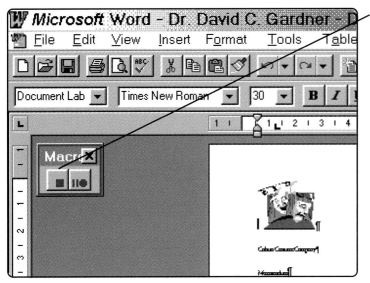

5. **Click** on the **Stop button** on the macro recorder toolbar. The macro recorder toolbar will disappear. All of the steps in the macro are now recorded.

6. **Click** on **File** in the menu bar. A pull-down menu will apppear.

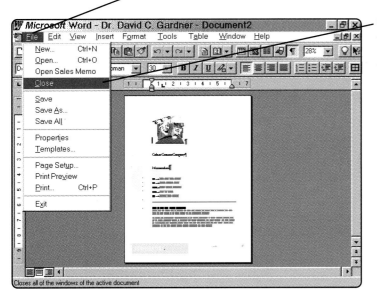

7. **Click** on **Close**. The Document1 screen will appear.

USING THE MACRO

1. **Click** on **File** in the menu bar. A pull-down menu will appear.

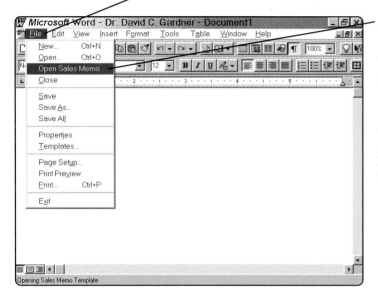

2. **Click** on **Open Sales Memo**. The Sales Memo will appear as Document3, ready for editing. Wow!

Note: The document number will depend on the number of documents you have already opened.

DELETING THE MACRO

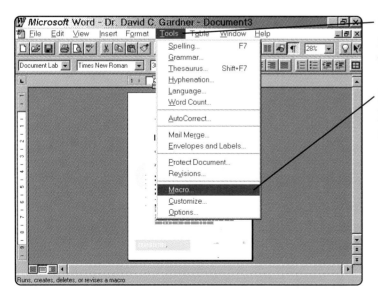

1. **Click** on **Tools** in the menu bar. The Tools menu will appear.

2. **Click** on **Macro**. The Macro dialog box will appear.

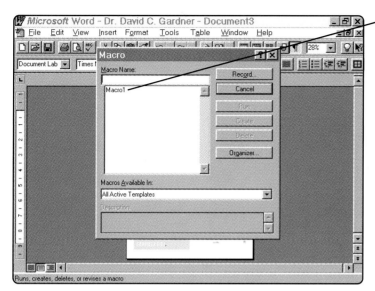

3. **Click** on **Macro1**. It will move to the Macro Name text box. The description of the Macro will appear in the Description text box.

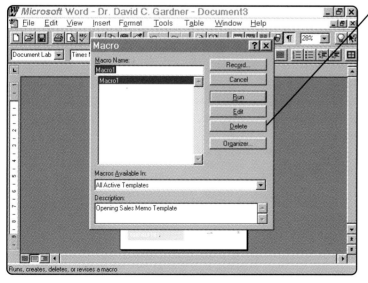

4. **Click** on **Delete**. A Microsoft Word dialog box will appear.

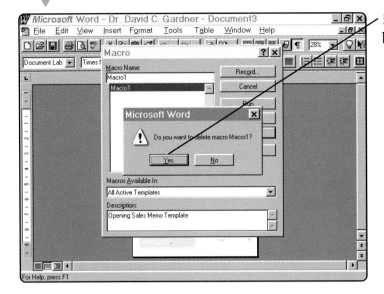

5. Click on **Yes.** The dialog box will close.

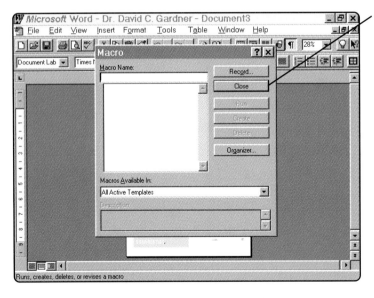

6. Click on **Close**. The dialog box will close.

EXITING WORD

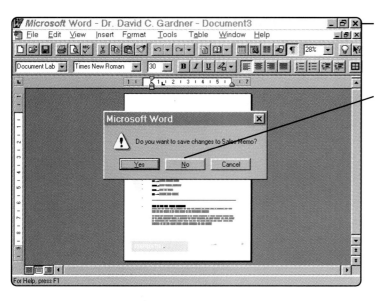

1. **Click** on the **Close Word button** on the title bar. A dialog box will appear.

2. **Click** on **No.**

WHAT NEXT ?

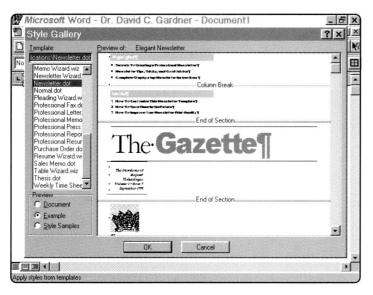

There are many exciting features of Word 7 left to explore. We hope this introduction has given you an understanding of its capabilities. We hope, also, that you have gained confidence in your ability to master its complexities. Experiment! Have fun!

WORD FOR WINDOWS 95

Part VI: Appendices

Appendix A: Installing Word 7 for Windows 95	Page 258
Appendix B: Hiding the Taskbar	Page 270

Installing Word 7 for Windows 95

Windows 95 has simplified the way you install programs. In fact, if your computer has a CD-Rom drive, the process is not only simple, it is *very* fast. In this chapter, you will do the following:

✔ Install Word 7 for Windows 95 as a part of the Microsoft Office installation

OPENING THE CONTROL PANEL

Before you can begin to install the Microsoft Office programs, you must open up the Control Panel.

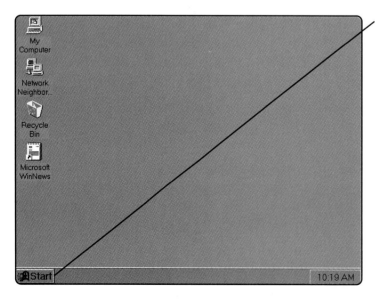

1. **Click** on the **Start button** in the taskbar. A pop-up menu will appear.

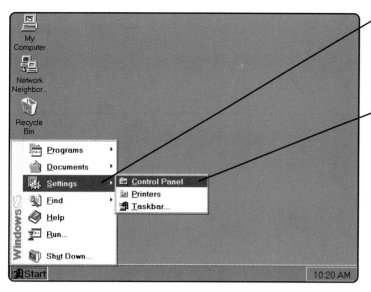

2. Move the mouse arrow up the menu to **Settings**. A second pop-up menu will appear.

3. Move the mouse arrow over to highlight **Control Panel**.

4. Click on **Control Panel**. The Control Panel dialog box will appear.

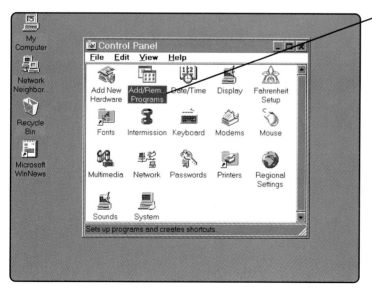

5. Click twice on **Add/Rem Programs**. The Add/Remove Programs Properties dialog box will appear.

INSTALLING A PROGRAM

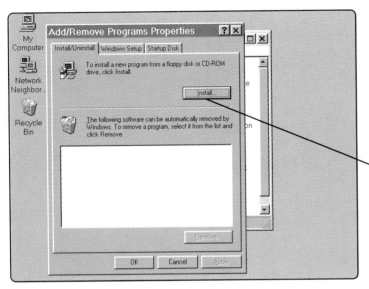

The following sections illustrate an installation using a CD-ROM disk. However, if you are using floppy disks for your installation, your screens will vary from these examples.

1. **Click** on the **Install button**. The Install Program From Floppy Disk or CD-ROM dialog box will appear.

2. **Insert** your **CD-ROM** disk into your CD-ROM drive.

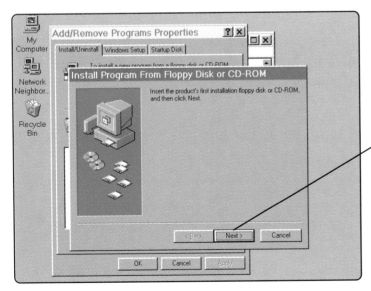

Remember, for some drives you may be required to place the CD-ROM disk into a special carrier before you insert the disk into the drive.

3. **Click** on **Next>**. Windows 95 will quickly read drive A and drive B as it searches for the installation program. Once Windows 95 finds the installation program disk in the CD-ROM drive, the Run Installation Program message box will appear.

Notice that the command line for the installation automatically appears in the text box.

4. **Click** on **Finish**. The Setup Message box will appear.

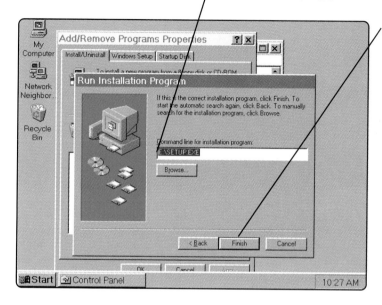

After a few minutes, the Microsoft Office 95 Setup message box will appear.

Next, a Microsoft Office '95 welcome message screen will appear.

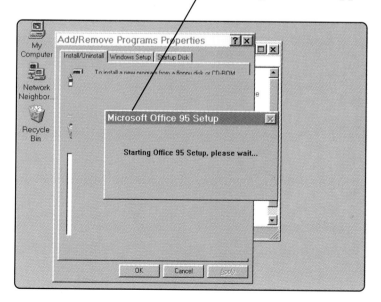

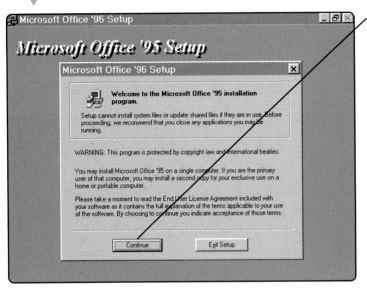

5. **Click** on **Continue**. The Name and Organization Information dialog box will appear.

Notice that the name and organization information used in registering Windows 95 automatically appears in the text box below.

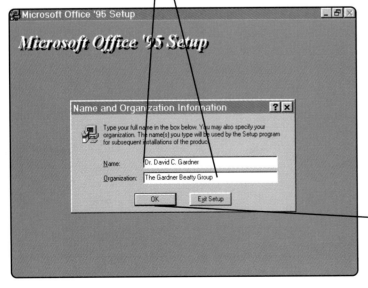

If this information is not correct, you can make the changes now. Or you can fill in new information (which will be used for subsequent installations of this product). Notice the cursor is flashing in the Name text box. When you start typing, the cursor will disappear.

6. **Click** on **OK**. Another Microsoft Office '95 message box will appear.

7. **Click** on **OK** if the information is correct. The Microsoft Office '95 Setup dialog box will appear.

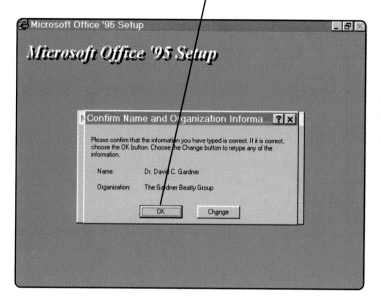

If the information is not correct, **click** on **Change**. The previous dialog box will appear. After making your corrections, **click** on **OK** to return to this message box.

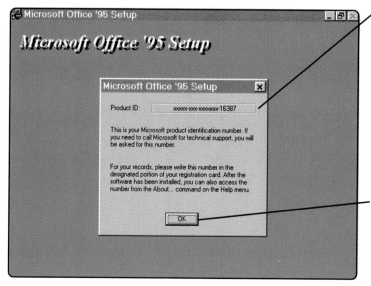

Notice that your registration number appears on this screen. It is important that you make a note of the number and keep it handy. If you call Microsoft for technical support, you will need this number for identification.

8. **Click** on **OK**.

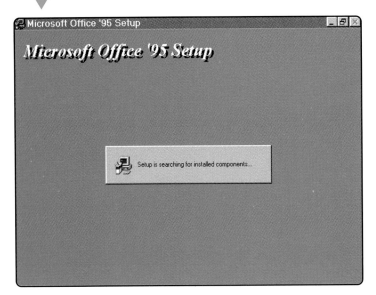

The hourglass will appear briefly along with a Microsoft message box that says "Setup is searching for installed components."

Selecting a Folder for OFFICE95

Microsoft Office will automatically be installed to a new folder (directory), OFFICE95, which will be created on the C drive (C:\OFFICE95).

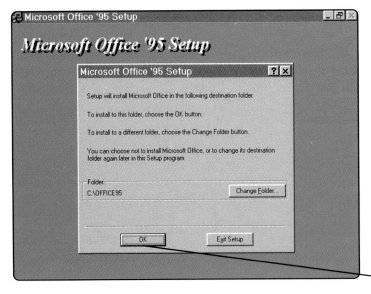

If, however, you wish to install this program in another directory (folder) or on another drive select the **Change Folder button**. A Change Directory dialog box will appear. **Type** in the new **folder (directory) name and path** and **click** on OK. A confirmation destination message box will appear. **Click** on **Yes** to confirm.

1. **Click** on **OK**. After a wait, a Microsoft Office dialog box will appear.

SELECTING PROGRAMS TO INSTALL

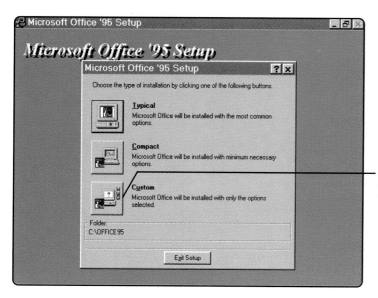

We recommend the Custom installation so that you can install Word's Clip Art. You can always add or remove programs and components at a later date by repeating the steps in this appendix.

1. **Click** on **Custom**. The Microsoft Office '95-Custom dialog box will appear.

2. **Click** in the **box** to *remove* the ✔ from any programs you *don't* want to install at this time.

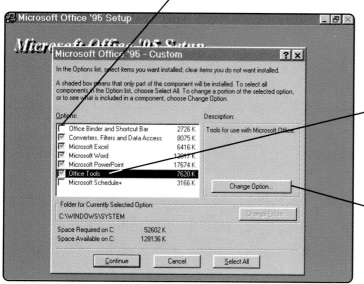

In this example, we won't install the Office Binder and Shortcut Bar, or the Microsoft Schedule+.

3. **Click** on the **words "Office Tools"** to highlight the line. *Don't* click on the box or you'll remove the ✔.

4. **Click** on **Change Option**. The Microsoft Office '95 - Office Tools dialog box will appear.

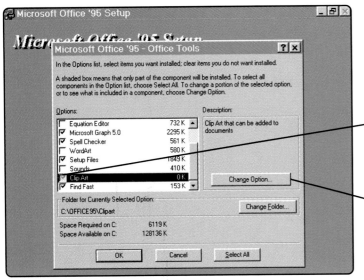

Adding ClipArt

1. **Click repeatedly** on the ▼ to scroll to the bottom of the Options list.

2. **Click** in the **box** to the left of **ClipArt** to place a ✔ in the box and highlight it.

3. **Click** on **Change Option**. The Microsoft Office 95-Clip Art dialog box will appear.

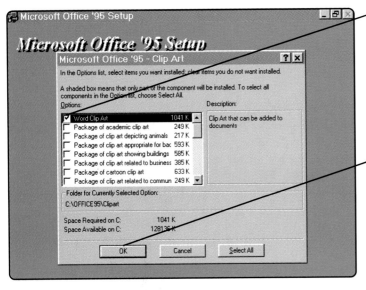

4. **Click** in the **box** to the left of **Word Clip Art** to place a ✔ in the box and highlight it.

Remember that you can add any or all of these clip art packages at any time.

5. **Click** on **OK**. The Clip Art dialog box will close.

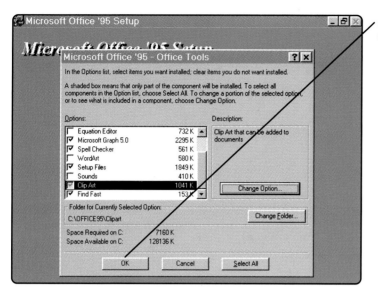

6. **Click** on **OK**. The Office Tools dialog box will close.

7. **Click** on **Continue**. The dialog box will close, and the Microsoft Office Setup: Disk 1 dialog box will appear.

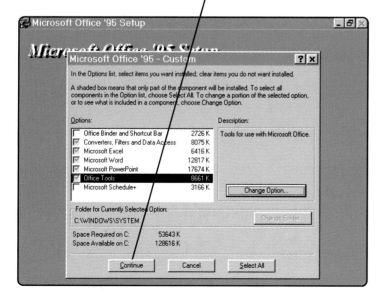

Watching, Waiting

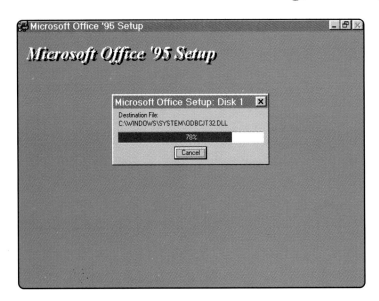

At this point sit back and relax. It's out of your hands. Using a CD-ROM certainly makes life easier. No more of the old "insert Disk #x" routine.

The Microsoft Office Setup: Disk 1 dialog box will show you the percentage of completion in copying files from the installation disk.

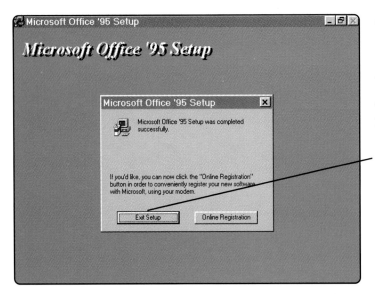

Closing the Installation

Looks like everything is complete, and you are nearly finished.

1. **Click** on **Exit Setup.** The setup will close, and the desktop will appear.

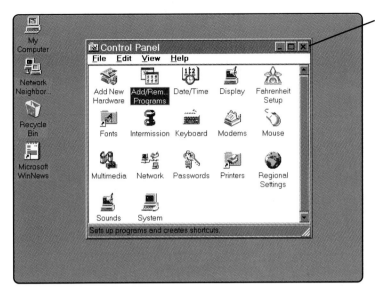

2. **Click** on the **Close button** (⊠) on the right side of the Control Panel title bar. The Control Panel window will close.

VIEWING MICROSOFT OFFICE

Now it's time to have fun exploring your new programs.

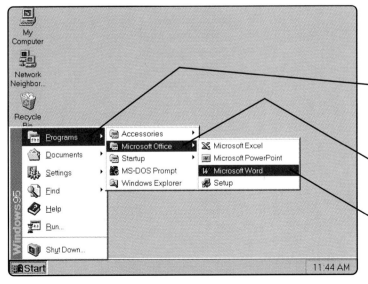

1. **Click** on the **Start button** on the taskbar. A pop-up menu will appear.

2. **Move** the **mouse arrow** up the menu to **Programs**. A second menu will appear.

3. **Move** the **mouse arrow** over to **Microsoft Office**.

4. **Move** the **mouse arrow** over to **Microsoft Word** and **click**.

Go to step 4 in the first section of Chapter 1, "Changing Margins and Fonts and Entering Text," to start with a screen that looks similar to this one.

Hiding the Taskbar

If you do not want the taskbar showing on your screen all the time, you can hide it from view and get it back anytime you need it with a simple mouse movement. In this chapter, you will do the following:

✔ "Hide" the taskbar
✔ Get the hidden taskbar back

REMOVING THE TASKBAR FROM VIEW

1. **Click** on **Start** in the left corner of the taskbar. A pop-up menu will appear.

2. **Move** the mouse arrow to **Settings.** Another menu will appear.

3. **Click** on **Taskbar**. The Taskbar Properties dialog box will appear.

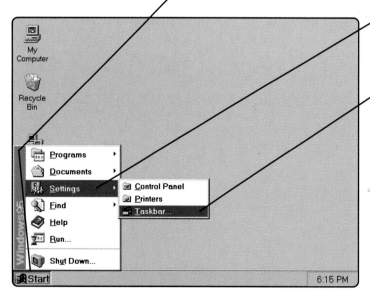

4. **Click** on **Always on top** to put a ✔ in the box if one isn't there already.

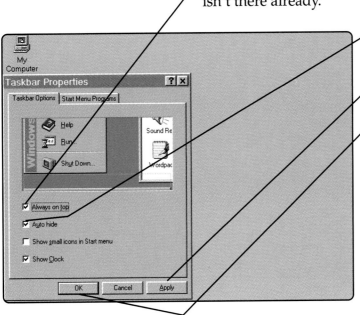

5. **Click** on **Auto hide** to put a ✔ in the box.

6. **Click** on **Apply**.

7. **Click on OK**. The dialog box will close.

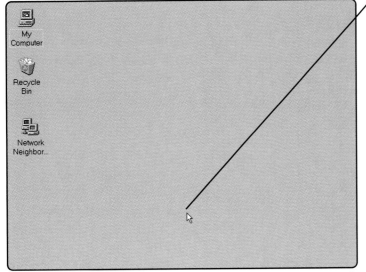

8. **Click anywhere** on the **desktop**. Voilà! The taskbar is gone.

So, how do you get it back when you need it? Go on to the next page.

GETTING THE HIDDEN
TASKBAR BACK

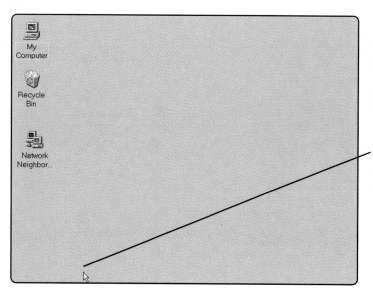

You can get the taskbar back anytime you want to by a simple mouse movement. You can do this at anytime from any program that you have running.

1. **Move** the **mouse arrow** towards the bottom of the desktop.

2. **Continue** to **move** the **mouse arrow** until the taskbar reappears.

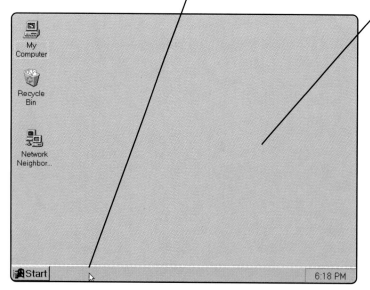

Note A: To hide the taskbar, simply move the mouse arrow up onto the desktop.

Note B: If you want to get the taskbar back permanently, repeat steps 1 to 6 in the first section of this chapter to remove the ✔ from the Auto hide box.

Index

NOTES

NOTES

NOTES

NOTES

NOTES

NOTES

NOTES

NOTES

NOTES

NOTES

NOTES